The Severn Bridge, gateway to Gwent and Wales.

Shire County Guide 15
GWENT

Anna Tucker

Shire Publications Ltd

CONTENTS

Set in 9 point Times roman and printed in Great Britain by C. I. Thomas & Sons (Haverfordwest) Ltd, Press Buildings, Merlins Bridge, Haverfordwest, Dyfed.

British Library Cataloguing in Publication Data available.

For Barley, who has yet to discover Gwent.

ACKNOWLEDGEMENTS
Photographs are acknowledged to: Cadbury Lamb, pages 2, 12, 44, 45 and 54; Anna Tucker, page 13. All the others, including the front cover, are by Paul Blyton. The map on page 63 is by Mr D. R. Darton.

COVER: The gatehouse on the Monnow Bridge at Monmouth.

BELOW: Junction Cottage, Pontymoel, on the Brecon and Abergavenny Canal.

Pollarded willows and reen on the coastal plain.

1
Introducing Gwent: landscape and history

Gwent is situated in the south-east corner of Wales. It is a county of some 530 square miles (1373 square kilometres), bounded on the east by the river Wye (which is also the boundary between England and Wales) and on the south by the Severn estuary. Visitors from southern England will reach the county by one of a number of dramatic crossing points: by road there is either the Severn Bridge or the elegant road bridge into Chepstow; by rail the Severn Tunnel or Brunel's railway bridge across the Wye.

The western and northern borders are less clearly defined by the geography of the area. On the west, the county border is formed partly by the river Rhymney (which flows into the Severn estuary near Cardiff) and partly by the ridge running between the Rhymney and Sirhowy valleys. To the north, the county stretches towards the Brecon Beacons and into the Black Mountains. The boundary runs eastwards from Rhyd-y-Milwr (where the counties of Powys, Mid Glamorgan and Gwent meet), over the Sugar Loaf mountain, projects a tongue northwards up the Vale of Ewyas to the ridge of the Black Mountains and then follows the river Monnow almost to the point where it flows into the Wye.

The county was formed in 1536 following the Act of Union between England and Wales. It was named Monmouthshire after the name of the town which stands at the confluence of the Monnow and the Wye. Monmouth is an abbreviation of Monnow-mouth, Monnow originally deriving from the Welsh *Myn-wy* (*myn*, swift; *wy*, water), thus combining both Welsh and English elements.

Monmouthshire was frequently but mistakenly regarded as an English county (perhaps in part because it was included on the

3

English court circuits); but English it is not and never was. Under local government reorganisation in 1974 the name was changed to Gwent, a reversion to a much older name which had originally applied to the district enclosed by the Usk, the Wye, the Monnow and the sea. The name probably derived from a word meaning open ground or plain. The kingdom of Gwent was divided into two areas, Gwent Iscoed (Gwent below the wood) and Gwent Uwchcoed (Gwent above the wood), also referred to as Overwent — a name which survives in Wentwood. To this area in 1536 was added the area of Gwynllwg, the region between the Rhymney and the Usk; the combination created the county boundaries which with a few minor alterations survive today.

Gwent is a county of varied and beautiful landscape, reflecting its position between the plains of England and the mountains of Wales. The county's character is determined by two principal geological features. Carboniferous rocks form a mountain and valley landscape in the west and in the south-east corner cause the spectacular gorge of the Wye valley. The remainder of the county is predominantly Old Red Sandstone of the Devonian era, except a small oval area around Usk where the rocks of this period have been worn away to reveal older Silurian rocks. The Old Red Sandstone engenders an undulating landscape covered with rich red soils rising to mountains in the north.

The southern fringe of the county bordering the Bristol Channel has been formed by rivers depositing mud and gravel to form a tract of low-lying ground known as the Caldicot and Wentloog levels. This strip of the county, which is 1 to 3 miles (2 to 5 km) wide and only a few feet above sea level, extends 24 miles (39 km) from Portskewett to Cardiff; throughout its length it is protected by a high sea wall and criss-crossed by drainage ditches or reens. This extensive drainage system has transformed unusable marsh into valuable agricultural land.

The west of the county stands in marked contrast to the coastal plains. Here the carboniferous rocks form an upland plateau deeply cut by parallel rivers flowing from north to south. These are the Rhymney, Sirhowy, Ebbw and Lwyd rivers, which have created steep-sided, V-shaped valleys before flowing into the Bristol Channel.

The eastern edge of this mountain area also runs approximately north to south from the hills overlooking Abergavenny to Risca. Besides containing iron and lead ores and coal measures, amongst the carboniferous rocks is limestone, which forms a narrow rim round the coalfields near Machen and Risca and proceeds north curving around the north

slopes of the Blorenge. The limestone strata have a steep westward dip of 20 to 60 degrees and contain many caverns well known by potholers for their linings of beautiful crystals of calcite and quartz. Above the carboniferous limestone lies millstone grit (so called because of its use in the manufacture of millstones). The upper part of the millstone grit has been named the 'Farewell Rock' because when coal miners reached it they knew it was useless to dig further in search of coal.

The coal measures to the west rest on the millstone grit and represent the most industrially valuable rocks in the county. They form part of the South Wales coalfield and are divided into Lower Coal measures, Pennant sandstones and Upper Coal measures. The lower measures contain most of the workable coal. The proximity of limestone (used as a flux allowing the smelting of iron at lower temperatures), iron ore, water and coal led to the early industrialisation of the valleys.

The Old Red Sandstone of the Devonian period forms most of the remaining part of the county. The beds stretch in an unbroken line from the Black Mountains, south past Monmouth and Abergavenny, encircling the Silurian rocks around Usk and extending to the south-west beyond Newport. In the centre and north of the county the beds undulate but near the Wye they dip steadily eastwards, passing under the carboniferous limestone series between Tintern and Chepstow, while in the west they dip westwards disappearing below the South Wales coalfield.

In the north of the county, between Monmouth and Abergavenny, the landscape is gently rolling but it rises to Old Red Sandstone peaks on the edges of the county. Pen-y-fal (better known as the Sugar Loaf), rising to 1955 feet (596 metres), and Skirrid Fawr, 1596 feet (486 metres), are near Abergavenny and Beacon Hill and the Kymin are near Monmouth. Further south is the flat basin of the Usk valley, which then rises to a stretch of wooded hills lying between Newport and Monmouth and known as Wentwood. This sandstone ridge rises to 1000 feet (305 metres) above sea level and commands magnificent views over the coastal plains to the south and the Bristol Channel beyond.

THE COASTAL PLAIN

Gwent does not have a coastline edged with sandy beaches but the coastal region does have its own unique character. The plains are bounded on one side by Wentwood ridge and on the other by the Severn estuary and are intersected by numerous ditches. It is reminiscent of the Dutch landscape, with few hedges as the water-filled ditches act as field boundaries. In past times it also had windmills to provide power for grinding corn, but these

4

Pen-y-fal (Sugar Loaf) from Skirrid Fawr.

have long since disappeared (the only windmill that remains to be seen in Gwent stands in ruins just to the north of Usk).

When the Romans came to Wales the plain must have been unusable marsh and bog but they realised its potential as rich agricultural land by building a sea wall to prevent incursions and draining the area by an intricate system of ditches known as reens. The coastal plain is divided into two parts by the Usk, which flows into the Severn estuary. To the east is Caldicot Level and to the west is Wentloog Level. In 1878 a slab of lias limestone was worn out of the sea wall near Goldcliff by the constant erosion of the tides. Inscribed on the stone in Latin is the information that 'the Century of Statorius Maximus in the First Cohort (built) 31½ paces'. Other inscriptions recording the working parties who built sections must be still contained within the wall. This stone is now in the Roman Legionary Museum at Caerleon.

On 20th January 1606 a disastrous flood was caused by a storm that raged from the southwest for three days, resulting in abnormal spring tides. The sea overflowed the protecting walls and flooded 26 parishes between Rumney and Mathern, causing devastation in loss of life and crops. A tablet in Goldcliff church records that 22 people were drowned in that parish alone.

Goldcliff gets its name from the appearance of the cliffs noted by Giraldus Cambrensis in the twelfth century. The cliffs are formed from grey marls, black shales and thin light-coloured limestones. The shales contain iron pyrites, conspicuous by its bright metallic lustre. When it reflected the sun it must indeed have seemed a 'gold cliff'. Unfortunately the phenomenon can no longer be seen, as the cliff is reinforced with limestone blocks to guard against erosion.

Many of the place-names in this area are of Saxon rather than Welsh origin, reflecting the pattern of early settlement. Along the coastline are a number of small inlets called 'pills'

5

Mural at Brynawel, showing Wakes Week celebrations.

which in previous times were used as small harbours. Salmon fishing takes place along the coast, making use of the large tidal fluctuations. Inland the area is a region of mixed farming.

In this area are the spectacular Severn Bridge, the Severn Tunnel (the longest main-line railway tunnel in Britain), and, near Newport, Llanwern Steelworks and the striking Inmos factory designed by Richard Rogers and Partners, as well as ancient manor houses, castles and churches.

THE FOUR INDUSTRIAL VALLEYS

The valleys of Gwent were described by W. J. Smart as having 'rows and rows of depressing dwellings where miners live; their children play in shabby streets; the wheels at the pitheads revolve pitilessly as men go to work in the dark underworld of dead forests, and when they come up again it is to look upon the black monstrous, menacing slag heaps rearing their hideous heads everywhere.' This is no longer true of this area as the traditional industries of iron and steel making and mining have all but disappeared.

The valleys are gradually returning to the more rural aspect which they had before the 1780s. However, the booming industrial years have left their mark. All the valleys are narrow and steeply sided, widening out gradually at the southern end. This has determined the shape of the towns, whose streets often run as terraces of houses ranked one above the other along the valley sides. Bricks, which were made to provide linings for blast furnaces,

6

quickly superseded stone as a building material so the valley towns are predominantly of red brick often with yellow brick or stone detailing.

The rapid industrial development necessitated good communications, resulting in canals, tramroads and railways which follow the geography of the area and run north to south. For those who are interested in industrial archaeology the area has a wealth of fascinating sites (see chapter 7), ranging from the Blaenavon Ironworks to industrial housing and the Clydach Valley, where nature has almost reclaimed her own, leaving only clues to the industrial past. This area is the setting for Alexander Cordell's book *Rape of the Fair Country*.

At Brynawel, where a new road has been constructed crossing the Sirhowy river, a mural was commissioned in celebration of the valley's industrial past and its people. It was designed by Kenneth and Oliver Budd in 1985 and depicts a colliery winding gear with men and horses working underground and the celebrations of a Wakes Week with a procession carrying chapel banners, rugby players, a band and a boxing competition.

Above the towns rear the mountainous moorland ridges which have continued to be used for sheep rearing. At Mynyddislwyn and Bedwellty one can gain some idea of what the villages and hamlets were like before industrialisation, with ancient parish churches. Gelligroes mill and Penllwyn Mawr manor, the ancestral home of the Morgan family, can also be found in these valleys. At the termination of the ridges overlooking Newport stands the county's most dramatic hillfort, Twm Barlwm (see chapter 3).

THE VALE OF USK

The Vale of Usk extends from where the river emerges from between the hills in the north of Gwent and flows south in a leisurely fashion through river meadows, rich pasture land and the towns of Abergavenny, Usk, Caerleon and Newport to the Bristol Channel. William Gilpin in his travels commented that 'the Usk continued, everywhere, our amusing companion: and if, at any time, it made a more devious curve than usual, we were sure to meet it again, at the next turn...'

On the west side it is overlooked by a ridge of hills around whose feet wends the Brecon and Abergavenny Canal. The Usk is too shallow in the north of the county to be navigable so the canal was constructed to move industrial and agricultural products.

It is a gentle countryside scattered with market towns and many attractive villages with castles and Norman earthworks. Because of its meanders the river is spanned by a good number of medieval stone bridges. This area had both good timber and Old Red Sandstone for building, but its old buildings are predominantly of stone and originally would have been roofed with stone slates. However, since the railways reached the area the most common roofing material has become slate. The district is well known for its old houses, many built by gentlemen farmers.

Among other buildings of interest in the vale are Clytha House and Castle. Clytha Castle is a folly built in 1790 by William Jones of nearby Clytha House in memory of his wife; 'it was undertaken for the purpose of relieving a mind sincerely afflicted by the loss of a most excellent wife'. It now belongs to the Landmark Trust and is rented out as self-catering holiday accommodation.

THE WYE VALLEY

The Wye Valley has been popular with tourists since the eighteenth century and has much more dramatic scenery than the equally beautiful Usk Valley. In Gwent the Wye runs from Monmouth to Chepstow, where it flows into the Severn estuary. It is bounded by the Forest of Dean on the English side and the hills of Wentwood on the Welsh.

The Wye is tidal in its lower reaches and so it is bordered by grey mud banks at low tide. Tennyson wrote in his poem *In Memoriam:*

'There twice a day the Severn fills,
The salt sea-water passes by,
And hushes half the babbling Wye
And makes a silence in the hills.'

The river was navigable as far as Hereford in flat-bottomed boats known as trows. It used to be busy with river craft carrying timber and oak bark and pleasure steamers filled with tourists but today is used only by a few private boats.

In this area one can explore the Kymin with the Round House and Naval Temple on top, the ruins of Tintern Abbey, Piercefield walks around Piercefield House, the Wyndcliff with its 365 steps and early industrial sites. There are also a number of interesting geological features: the Devil's Pulpit (see chapter 9), the Suck Stone, a huge piece of conglomerate rock (OS 162, SO 538142), and the Buck Stone (OS 162, SO 543123), which have been left standing out by the erosion of the softer rocks around them. The Buck Stone used to rock on its base but was completely overturned in 1885. The people in the neighbourhood were so upset that the stone had to be re-set in its former position, but secured so that it no longer moves.

Many of the villages in the valley were formerly industrial; at Whitebrook there were wireworks and pinmaking and the pounds which provided the water power have been landscaped into lakes in private gardens. It is difficult to imagine in the present rural calm the industry which was recorded by Edward Davies in the eighteenth century. Tintern he described thus:

'Black forges smoke and noisy hammers beat,
Where sooty cyclops, puffing, drink and sweat.'

Particularly around Tintern the narrow valley is dotted with hotels, guest houses and tourist shops. At Tintern Parva on a steep south-facing hill slope is one of Gwent's two vineyards (the other is near Monmouth), which offers guided tours to visitors.

WENTWOOD

Wentwood is an upland area, the highest point of the ridge reaching 989 feet (301 metres). Pen-y-cae-mawr rises to 950 feet (290 metres), Chepstow Park Wood 932 feet (284 metres) and Gray Hill (or Mynydd Lwyd) 902 feet (275 metres), with its twin hill Mynydd Allt Tir Bach 791 feet (241 metres). Vantage points within the area provide good views of the county. From the Usk to Chepstow road, as it climbs on to the ridge one can look north across the Vale of Usk, with its quilted pattern of fields, to the mountains on the fringes of the county. From the summit of Gray Hill one can survey the coastal plains, the hilly ridge extending towards Cardiff in the west and towards Gloucestershire in the east, with the counties of south-west England lying beyond the Bristol Channel.

In medieval times it was a densely forested area. Forests were a valuable source of profit and were jealously protected by the Crown. Wentwood was administered by the Lord of Striguil. Local people had certain rights, to cut timber for house building and fencing, to collect brushwood for fuel, and pannage for pigs. These fed on acorns, hazel and beech nuts and were charged for at 2d per head.

The indigenous forest, predominantly of oak, was cleared over the centuries and parts have now been replanted with conifers by the Forestry Commission. Wentwood was an important source of timber for boatbuilding right up to the Second World War.

Today it is a pleasant region scattered with many villages and hamlets, some remote and isolated along leafy lanes, all of them picturesquely sited. There are signs of early occupation in the form of stone circles, standing stones and hillforts. Near Newchurch can be found Castell Troggy, a ruined castle built towards the end of the thirteenth century as an outpost guarding the boundaries of Striguil.

The area is well served by numerous footpaths and picnic sites and is good for woodland and hill walking, with Wentwood Reservoir providing a focal point.

THE BLACK MOUNTAINS AND THREE PEAKS

This area is on the northern fringes of the county and forms part of the Brecon Beacons National Park surrounding Abergavenny. It is very different from the rest of the county as the landscape on the tops of the hills is mountainous and moor-like. The hills are formed from Old Red Sandstone often topped with 'brown stone', which is slightly more resistant to erosion.

The area shows signs of glaciation from the last ice age. The sides of the Blorenge have been scooped out by ice action to form cwms. The peak of the Sugar Loaf, which appears to be almost volcanic in shape from the north and south, is a short ridge sculpted by parallel glaciers. The Llanthony valley is a glaciated U-shaped valley.

The valley bottoms are used predominantly for mixed pastoral farming and the mountains for sheep grazing. The hilltops are scattered with cairns and the south facing ridges terminating the Black Mountains are occupied by iron age hillforts. On the summit of Skirrid Fawr once stood a Roman Catholic chapel dedicated to St Michael. The only remains to be seen are two upright stones where the entrance used to be.

The area is popular for walking, pony trekking, fishing and boating and is ideal for the more recent sport of hang-gliding. The two sites frequently used are the Blorenge, spiralling down into the Castle Meadows beside the Usk at Abergavenny, and the Hatterall Ridge bordering Herefordshire.

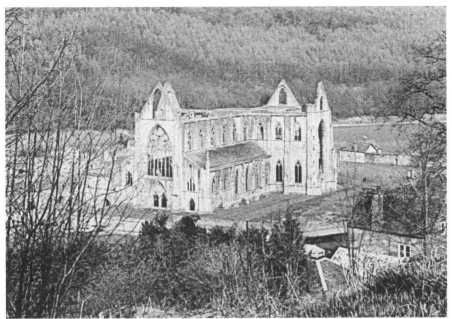

Tintern Abbey in the Wye Valley.

2
Exploring the Gwent countryside

Gwent is a county well worth exploring on foot or by car. Many small car parks or viewpoints have been created which either make a good place from which to start a walk or provide spectacular vistas across the county for those who wish to sit and contemplate.

Many people will prefer to find their own way around the county with the aid of Ordnance Survey maps, which show public footpaths. However, this chapter suggests a wide range of ideas for exploring the varied landscape of Gwent. Gwent County Council Planning Department produces a number of leaflets about walks in the county and can be contacted at County Hall, Cwmbran; telephone Cwmbran (063 33) 67711. Guided walks are also organised and information about these can be obtained from the same source.

There are several country parks in the county. Some of them are associated with historic buildings such as Caldicot Castle Country Park and Tredegar House and Country Park (see chapter 6). There are numerous picnic areas with car parks which form the starting points for nature trails and walks. These are recommended both for walkers and for brief stops during a car tour.

Abbey Tintern Furnace Trail, Tintern (OS 162; SO 514003).

The Abbey Tintern Furnace Trail is a reminder of the Wye Valley area's industrial past. It is situated in the Angidy valley, where fast running water supplied power for wiremaking. A furnace established about 1600 supplied iron to the wireworks.

Beaufort Aviaries, Devauden Green, near Chepstow.

The aviaries are set in attractive gardens at Devauden Green on the B4293 4 miles (6 km) from Chepstow. Exotic, brightly coloured birds to see include unusual pheasants, parakeets and peacocks.

Brecon and Abergavenny Canal.

The towpath of the Brecon and Abergavenny Canal provides an easy-to-follow long walk with no hills. It takes a slightly elevated course, so providing fine views across the county. It is frequently crossed by high arching stone bridges and there are a number of boat yards, wharves and canal keepers' cottages along its banks.

9

The Abergavenny and Border Counties Show with the Blorenge in the background.

The Brecon Beacons National Park. National Park Office, 2 Lower Monk Street, Abergavenny. Telephone: Abergavenny (0873) 3254.

The Brecon Beacons National Park covers substantial areas beyond the boundaries of Gwent, but within the county it extends a finger southwards to include the area between the Usk and Torfaen valleys, crosses the river at Llanfoist and incorporates all the hills to the north and west of Abergavenny.

On the summit of the Blorenge are a number of viewpoints. One of the most popular is the area around **Pen-ffordd-goch Pond,** better known as Keeper's Pond. It was constructed in the 1820s to supply water to the forges at Garnddyrys, approximately a mile north, where slag from the works can still be seen. The village which housed the workers has completely disappeared.

On the east side of the **Blorenge** are two small viewpoints, one (OS 161, SO 271101) looks south down a steep valley and the other, further along the same road (OS 161, SO 282112), has magnificent views to the east and Skirrid Fach and Fawr. Also on the Blorenge is the **Foxhunter car park** (OS 161, SO 265110), where a plaque marks the grave of

Foxhunter, the famous showjumping horse owned by Lieutenant Colonel Harry Llewellyn and ridden by him in the Olympic Games of 1948 and 1952, on the latter occasion winning a gold medal as a member of the victorious British team.

The **Sugar Loaf** or Pen-y-Fal is also a popular place for locals and visitors alike. Walkers can reach the summit from two car parks. One is sited on top of Llanwenarth Breast (OS 161, SO 267170), overlooking the Usk Valley, while the other looks down on Abergavenny from Porth-y-parc (OS 161, SO 288166). The other summit to be climbed is **Skirrid Fawr,** which can be reached from a lay-by on the B4521 (OS 161, SO 331165).

Broadmeend Forest Trail, near Trelleck (OS 162; SO 505043).

Broadmeend Forest Trail is a nature reserve including Cleddon Bog. There are plants and wildlife associated with wetland areas. Permission must be obtained from County Hall, Cwmbran (see page 9).

Clytha Picnic Site (OS 161; SO 362085). National Trust. Walks from here can be enjoyed along the river Usk or a more

10

strenuous walk leads to the summit of Coed-y-Bwnydd, where there is an impressive hillfort.

Cwmcarn Forest Drive, Cwmcarn (OS 171; ST 233935). Off the A467 west of Cwmcarn. Forestry Commission.

Cwmcarn Forest Drive starts at a visitor centre, where information about walks can be collected. There is a 7 mile (11 km) drive through the Ebbw Forest, which covers 11,100 acres (4492 ha), with parking spots, picnic areas and viewpoints. It is a twentieth-century commercial forest where planting first began in the 1920s and recreates in part the ancient forest of Machen. There is a variety of trees including Japanese larch, grand and noble firs, Scots pine, Sitka spruce and naturally grown deciduous trees which are not to be felled commercially. The timber is often used as pit props in the local collieries as well as for pulp and fibre board.

There are many footpaths which lead out on to the mountain tops over 1300 feet (400 metres) above sea level, with spectacular views over the Bristol Channel and beyond. Twm Barlwm (see chapter 3) can be reached from car park 2 or a steeper climb from car park 7.

Cwmtillery Lake Picnic Site, North of Abertillery (OS 161; SO 218062).

The lake is a good starting point for mountain walks.

The Kymin, Monmouth (OS 162; SO 527123). National Trust.

The Kymin is a hill overlooking Monmouth. A number of footpaths lead to its summit, which can also be reached by car. On top stands the Round House, built in 1793, where Monmouth gentlemen could dine and which was visited by Lord Nelson in 1802. Nearby is the Naval Temple, which was erected in 1800 to commemorate the victories of naval commanders and is dedicated to the Duchess of Beaufort, daughter of Admiral Boscawen.

Llandegfedd Farm Park, Llandegfeth, Newport.

The farm park has displays of farm machinery, unusual breeds of farm animals and an adventure playground.

Llandegfedd Reservoir, (OS 171; ST 325995).

Llandegfedd Reservoir is the largest reservoir in the county and is popular for fishing, sailing, wind-surfing and birdwatching. There are a number of walks between 2 and 5½ miles (3-9 km) in length starting from the reservoir or Sor Brook picnic area.

Mountain Air Picnic Site, Between Upper Cwmbran and Pontypool (OS 171; SO 274968).

This is an ideal starting place for climbing the slopes of Mynydd Maen.

Offa's Dyke Path

This long-distance path runs along the English side of the Wye with fine views over Gwent and enters the county just north of Redbrook before climbing to the top of the Kymin. The entire length from South to North Wales is about 170 miles (274 km), of which about 20 miles (32 km) run through Gwent. The dyke was never constructed in Gwent so the path follows a varied course through Monmouth and across the rolling farmlands of north-east Gwent before climbing the Hatterall and following the eastern ridge of the Black Mountains and leaving the county just beyond Llanthony Abbey.

Pen-y-fan Pond Country Park, near Crumlin (OS 171; ST 195005). Just north of the B4251.

The pond was constructed in the 1790s to augment the water supply to the Monmouthshire Canal and now provides the focal point of the park.

Sirhowy Valley Country Park. Visitor centre at the Babell Chapel, Cwmfelinfach (OS 171, ST 183922).

The park covers an area of 1000 acres (400

Naval Temple and Round House on the Kymin near Monmouth.

ha) of outstanding natural beauty with two picnic sites and a series of walks. For those who are unable or unwilling to walk, Land Rover safaris are available. There is also a fitness circuit with twelve stations featuring different exercise apparatus.

Tintern Station Picnic Area, Tintern (OS 162; SO 537006).

This is no longer a working railway station but an interpretative centre with facilities for school visits, an exhibition area and marked walks, some with firm level surfaces ideal for elderly or disabled visitors.

Usk Valley Walk

This long-distance footpath is just over 25 miles (40 km) long and runs from the Ship Inn at Caerleon (OS 171; ST 342902) to the Usk Bridge at Abergavenny (OS 161; SO 292139). For long sections it follows the banks of the river but it also leads through fields and woods, along country lanes, through hamlets and villages and passes Kemeys' Folly and Llancayo windmill along the way. The route is

waymarked with yellow arrows with yellow dots on a black background.

Wentwood Reservoir, near Llanvair Discoed (OS 171; ST 429937).

A picnic site on Forestry Commission land overlooks the reservoir, a beautiful 40 acre (16 ha) fishing lake.

Wye Valley Walk

The Wye Valley Walk, a long-distance path, is waymarked with yellow arrows. It begins at Chepstow Castle and follows the west bank of the Wye through the walks created as part of the park of Piercefield House. The path follows the Wye to Monmouth and then leaves Gwent to continue to Ross-on-Wye (34 miles, 55 km) and beyond.

The Wyndcliff, St Arvans (OS 162; SO 525973).

The Wyndcliff, with its 365-step climb, provides marvellous views and can be reached from car parks and picnic sites sited west of the A466 (OS 162; SO 525973). The steps were constructed in 1828 by the Duke of Beaufort's steward, Osmond Wyatt.

Tintern Station Picnic Area.

12

Gaer Llwyd burial chamber.

3
Places of archaeological interest

Evidence of stone age man is found throughout the county. This was a period when man was a nomadic hunter and fisher following herds of game and living in the natural shelter of caves, where these were to be found. Animal bones and stone artefacts were found at the Doward caves on the Gloucestershire side of the River Wye and are now in the museum at Monmouth.

There are no early stone age (palaeolithic) sites to be visited but stone and fliint tools which have been found can be seen at Abergavenny, Monmouth and Newport museums and at the National Museum of Wales. At Newport Museum can be seen human skeletal remains probably of neolithic date found at Ifton Quarries and a human cranium and animal remains of a similar period found during the construction of the New Docks in Newport.

During the neolithic period man was becoming more settled and a more sophisticated society was evolving from which more evidence survives. The burial places of the dead are monuments of this period. For many years these megalithic tombs were regarded as druids' altars and because it was not known how they had come about many fantastic legends grew up around them. The earliest and simplest tomb was a chamber formed of three

or more upright stones with a capstone placed on top. This structure was covered with a mound of earth, stones and sods which has eroded over the centuries, leaving only the stones. Gwent has three chambered tombs, Gaer Llwyd, Heston Brake and Gwern-y-Cleppa.

There are also numerous standing stones in the county, the best known being Harold's Stones at Trelleck and the Druidstone near Castleton.

The unwary must beware as there are a number of stone circles in the county which were erected (as they were throughout Wales) where a National Eisteddfod has been held. There is one just outside Abergavenny alongside the A40 erected in 1913 and another in Pontypool Park dating from 1924.

A prehistoric trackway has been found in the intertidal areas of the river Severn near Magor. To prevent its destruction by tidal action sections of the track were salvaged and when preservation is completed they will be displayed in Newport Museum.

The bronze age is the name given to the era from about 2000 BC to 800 BC, in which early man was beginning to work in metal although flint and stone tools and weapons continued to be used. A very finely worked flint arrowhead from this period can be seen in Abergavenny

13

Museum. During this period pottery of the distinctive beaker type was often left with burials in round barrows. In the middle of this period cremation of the dead instead of inhumation became the practice. Cremation ashes were buried in a vessel together with food vessels and other grave goods.

Numerous bronze axes have been discovered as stray finds and can be seen in the county's museums and the National Museum of Wales. Several hoards have also been discovered. One was found north-west of St Andrew's church, Beaufort, in July 1922 which included several socketed axes and one palstave; another, of seven socketed axes, was found at Liveoaks Farm, St Arvans.

Round barrow burial sites can be found all over the hilltops of Gwent, those in the valley bottoms having been destroyed by agriculture. They are marked on the maps as 'cairns' or 'garns' and are recorded in such names as Garnddyrus near Blaenavon or Carn Defaid in the Torfaen valley, where human remains were interred in a central cist.

The term 'iron age' is given to the period from about 800 BC to 43 AD, when the technology of ironworking had been introduced to Britain by European immigrants. The most imposing monuments left by the peoples of this era are the hillforts, of which there are over forty examples on the county's hilltops.

Documented history begins with the Roman invasion in AD 43. The Romans remained in occupation for nearly 400 years and although this was a short period compared with earlier invasions they left a considerable mark on the county.

Although the Romans conquered England and lowland Wales they had little success against the Welsh tribes who retreated into the mountains. The Romans decided to consolidate their empire by strongly fortifying the border area which ran through Gwent. Forts were established one day's march from each other at Caerleon (*Isca*), Usk (*Burrium*), Abergavenny (*Gobannium*) and Monmouth (*Blestium*).

Isca was the fortress of the Second Augustan Legion. The other forts were manned by auxiliary forces and were neither as extensive nor as substantially built. Roman remains are to be seen at Caerleon and at Caerwent, a Roman civil town. Military roads joining the forts were constructed and military leaders built villas outside the camps, so the county is rich in Roman remains. Artefacts can be seen in the local museums and the National Museum of Wales.

In the following gazetteer of ancient sites the relevant Ordnance Survey 1 : 50,000 map sheet number and the National Grid reference are given for each.

Caerleon legionary fortress (Isca), Caerleon (OS 171; ST 338906).

The most impressive remains are the **amphitheatre,** which stood outside the south-west entrance of the fort. It is oval in plan, 267 by 222 feet (81 by 68 metres), and built in stone. It was constructed towards the end of the first century AD, with later rebuildings. It had eight vaulted entrances, the two at either end being wide enough to admit chariots. The audience was seated on wooden benching banked up in tiers and it would probably have seated about 6000 people. Gladiatorial contests were staged to entertain the garrison. Adjacent to the western entrance is a building which is presumed to have confined wild beasts used in the ring.

A short walk from the amphitheatre can be seen the remains of the legionary **barracks.** The legionary soldiers lived here in ten large buildings. There was a parade ground where the playing fields of the comprehensive school are now sited. Near the Bull Inn, not far from the museum, are the **bath buildings.** They are the most complete example of a legionary bath building in Britain and were excavated in 1977-9. The remains are now protected from the elements by a modern building opened in 1985. Walkways have been constructed so visitors can overlook the baths once used by gladiators, athletes and Roman soldiers.

See chapter 6 for the Roman Legionary Museum.

Caerwent Roman town (Venta Silurum), Caerwent (OS 171; ST 468905).

At Caerwent it is the **Roman walls** of the town which have survived. In subsequent centuries Caerwent has been little more than a village so later building has not plundered or destroyed the Roman remains. The wall is traceable all round and parts can be easily viewed. Originally the wall would have stood about 17 feet (5.2 metres) high but it is still impressive today where in parts it reaches 15 feet (4.6 metres). It is between 7 and 8 feet (2.1 and 2.4 metres) wide and small guardrooms are interspersed along its length. The walls enclose an area of about 44 acres (18 ha), which is only slightly smaller than Caerleon.

The Druidstone, near Castleton (OS 171; ST 241834).

The Druidstone is an upright slab 10 feet (3.0 metres) high and 7 feet (2.1 metres) wide. It may be the remains of a neolithic chambered tomb although there are no signs of an earthen mound.

Gaer Llwyd, near Newchurch (OS 171; ST 447968). Just off the B4235.

This is the most complete megalithic tomb in

The Roman walls of Venta Silurum (Caerwent).

Gwent. The five supporting stones are *in situ* and the capstone, which is broken, is perilously perched on top of them. The construction of such a tomb must have been a great undertaking as the capstones can weigh as much as 40 tons.

Gray Hill, near Llanvair Discoed (OS 171; ST 437935).

On the summit of the Hill there are a number of stones which appear to be a circle but might also be the remains of several tombs.

Gwern-y-Cleppa, west of Newport (OS 171; ST 276851).

This megalithic tomb can be seen from the M4. The oval mound was orientated east to west and has three uprights remaining but the capstone has fallen and is now partially buried.

Harold's Stones, Trelleck (OS 162; SO 499051).

These three neolithic standing stones are located a few yards south of the B4293.

Heston Brake tomb, near Portskewett. (OS 162; ST 506887).

This megalithic tomb was investigated in 1889 and was found to have had two half-buried chambers placed end to end, both lacking capstones. A few human bones and fragments of pottery were found.

Llanmellin hillfort, near Caerwent (OS 171; ST 461926).

This iron age hillfort was investigated in 1930, when human and animal bones were found, together with pottery, fragments of bronze bracelets and a bronze brooch. The fort is in two parts, one enclosure of 5½ acres (2.2 ha) and another, somewhat later, of 2¼ acres (0.9 ha) divided into three compartments protected by a series of earth banks and ditches. It was possibly a centre of the Silures tribe which was abandoned when the Romans invaded the area.

Twm Barlwm hillfort, near Risca (OS 171; ST 243926).

Twm Barlwm is the most visible iron age hillfort in the county as it can be seen from the M4. The earthworks date from 1000 to 100 BC and represent the incomplete perimeter of a planned settlement (with a castle mound of 1500 years later at one end of the site). The unfinished defences show how the construction was organised by different gangs digging equal lengths.

Twyn-y-Gaer hillfort, near Cwmyoy (OS 161; SO 294214).

Twyn-y-Gaer, on the south-east ridge terminating the Llanthony valley, is the most extensively excavated hillfort in the county. It is oval in shape, with three enclosures protected by a rampart and ditch. Inside, the doorposts of timber-built houses have been discovered. Objects found include brooches, carpenters' and smiths' tools, slingstones and saddle and beehive querns. The finds are now in the National Museum of Wales. The fort was occupied from about 500 BC until the Roman invasion.

4
Castles

Gwent straddles areas of lowland and upland Wales and lies on the border of territories conquered by the Normans, who built a chain of castles along the border from the south to the north of Wales. The first to be built in Gwent was Chepstow Castle. The Normans were unable to subjugate the Welsh, who retreated into the hills; hence castles are to be found only in the eastern part of the county and along the southern coastline.

Almost every hamlet and village had some defence, usually a motte and bailey constructed in timber. As the Norman power became established these were abandoned and only castles of the greatest strategic importance were rebuilt and strengthened in stone. Today the remains of the abandoned mottes can be seen in the form of an artificial mound too steep to be cultivated and often topped with trees and brambles.

A number of castles have been converted into private houses, such as Usk Castle, or stand in ruins on private land, such as Castell Troggy. However, Gwent still has several castles which stand magnificent even in ruin as a reminder of the county's turbulent past and Norman authority in the area. Most of them are now administered by Cadw, Welsh Historic Monuments. Where a castle can be visited at any time, this is mentioned in the text. The other castles have fixed visiting hours and a charge is levied.

Abergavenny Castle, Abergavenny. Telephone: Abergavenny (0873) 4282. Monmouth District Council (unlimited visiting).

Little survives today of what was an important Norman stronghold. The castle was established by Hamelin de Ballon in about 1090 on a low hill left by the retreating glaciers in the valley of the river Usk. It is a strategic site occupied by the Romans nearly a thousand years earlier. The castle is at the highest point of the hill, with the Usk protecting its south-west flank and the Gavenny protecting the west side.

The ruins that can be seen today date from the twelfth to the fourteenth centuries, when the castle was built in stone, strengthened and enlarged. A range of buildings runs from the gatehouse, with a high section of curtain wall containing a first-floor great hall on the inside, to two towers, one octagonal and one circular, which would have contained the domestic apartments of the lord and his family. Surviving accounts dating from 1256-7 mention other buildings within the castle. For example, a pair of manacles, costing 6d, were purchased for

the prison and peacock feathers were used to decorate the chapel.

Abergavenny Castle was the scene of an atrocity perpetrated by William de Broase against his turbulent Welsh neighbours. De Broase invited Welsh chieftains to a banquet and once there he asked them to take an oath 'that no traveller by the waie amongst them should beare any bow or any other unlawful weapon'. This they refused to do, whereupon de Broase had his knights slaughter them. A few escaped and the Normans went after them to Castell Arnallt, where Sitsyllt lived, and slew his son and razed the place to the ground. Several years later the Welsh took their revenge and captured Abergavenny Castle.

In 1450 the Lordship of Abergavenny passed to the Nevill family, who still own the castle and lease it to the council. They were responsible for building the 'Keep' in 1819 as a private residence, part of which is now used as a museum (see chapter 7).

Caldicot Castle, Caldicot. Telephone: Caldicot (0291) 420241. Monmouth District Council.

In 1086 the Domesday Survey records Caldicot as being held for the King by the Sheriff of Gloucester, Durand. It was possibly his nephew Walter Fitzroger who began the castle by building a keep (later rebuilt in stone) on a high mound. The curtain walls, south-east and south-west towers were added later in the twelfth century by the de Bohun family, who also built the gate tower in the west wall.

The castle is 2 miles (3 km) from the sea and stands on flat land. Originally it was protected by a moat that could have been filled with water from the Nedern brook which flows on its east side.

In 1382-8 Thomas Woodstock and his wife, Alianore, built the square Woodstock Tower and the large gatehouse which is now used as the entrance. It is flanked with strong turrets and had a double portcullis.

The castle was maintained in good repair by its tenants under the Duchy of Lancaster until 1507. From then until 1830 it was leased as an agricultural holding only. The towers began to fall into ruin and by the eighteenth century the castle was overgrown and considered a romantic site worth visiting.

The castle was purchased by J. R. Cobb in 1885. He restored and rebuilt parts of the castle so that he and his family could live there. The most extensive rebuilding was the part of the gatehouse in red brick. The Cobb family remained until 1963, when it was purchased by Chepstow Rural District Council. The separate parts of the castle now house museum displays (see chapter 6).

Chepstow Castle, Chepstow. Telephone: (029 12) 4065. Cadw.

Chepstow Castle is strategically and scenically sited on the top of the cliffs overlooking the river Wye. It stands on a narrow spur which slopes down towards the river on the east. On the south side it is separated from the town by a broad deep gully now known as the Dell. The builders ingeniously used this strong natural position, which dictates the long and narrow layout of the castle.

The castle was begun by William Fitz Osbern, who died in 1071 and was one of William the Conqueror's staunch supporters. He was pushing the frontiers of the Norman conquest further west and Chepstow Castle was founded to fortify this boundary. The rectangular Great Tower was built on the narrowest part of the ridge and dates from about 1067-72, making Chepstow the earliest castle in Gwent.

In 1189 it passed by marriage to William Marshall, Earl of Pembroke. He considerably extended the castle by building a curtain wall which divided the middle from the lower bailey. Over the next 25 years, when William was succeeded by his five sons, the castle was enlarged and strengthened. The Great Tower was refashioned, the middle bailey was strengthened by the addition of a flanking tower and the curtain wall was largely rebuilt. The upper bailey was refashioned with a rectangular tower to command its western

gateway and later the barbican was rebuilt. The Marshalls also added the lower bailey with its formidable double-towered gatehouse.

The castle then passed into the hands of Roger Bigod, second Earl of Norfolk, followed by his son, Richard, in 1270. He built the Port Wall which protects the town and between 1278 and 1285 a new range of domestic buildings was constructed on the north side of the lower bailey. The south-east tower, now known as Marten's Tower (see chapter 8), was completed in 1293 and the remaining part of the upper storey of the Great Tower was finished. Apart from minor alterations, the castle was then essentially as we see it today.

During the Civil War the castle played an important role. At first it was held by Royalist forces but it was surrendered to Colonel Morgan of Gloucester following a four-day siege. On the outbreak of further hostilities in 1647 it was again controlled by the King's followers, under Sir Nicholas Kemeys. The Roundheads laid siege in May 1648 and the walls were breached by cannon near Marten's Tower. Sir Nicholas was killed and the garrison surrendered.

Following the Civil War the castle did not immediately fall into decay. In 1660, at the Restoration, Charles II handed it back to Lord Herbert, son of the rightful owner. It continued to be occupied by a garrison and it was used as a prison for political and military prisoners until the end of the seventeenth century.

The gatehouse of Chepstow Castle.

17

Grosmont Castle, Grosmont. Cadw (unlimited visiting). Telephone: Cardiff (0222) 465511.

Grosmont Castle is approached by a narrow lane leaving the main street of the village opposite the post office. On one side the land falls away to the river Monnow. It is protected all around by a deep moat, its grassy slopes studded with primroses in the spring.

A footbridge now crosses the moat where once there would have been a drawbridge. Although it was established as an early stronghold against the recurring attacks of the Welsh and was one of the so-called Trilateral Castles (the other two being Skenfrith and White Castle), in later years Grosmont Castle developed more comfortable residential quarters.

It is a compact castle, irregularly shaped but almost pentagonal in plan. On the right as you enter is the oldest part, believed to be the work of Hubert de Burgh, about 1200-4. It was a hall and private chamber, originally incorporated within the early timber defences. Later, when the outer defences were replaced in stone, about 1219-32, it was adapted to form service rooms and chambers to a new hall (now vanished) inside the courtyard.

On the opposite side of the curtain wall there are three large towers, two connected by the curtain wall. The third tower on the north side has a chimney shaft dating from the fourteenth century and still in good condition.

Between 1265 and the early fourteenth century Grosmont Castle passed from Edmund Crouchback, Earl of Lancaster, to his son Henry and then to his grandson, also Henry, who became Duke of Lancaster. His daughter married John of Gaunt and their son later became Henry IV.

The castle saw a number of skirmishes and was involved in the power struggle between Henry III and the barons. In 1233 Prince Llewellyn laid siege to it but was frightened off by the arrival of the King's army. Later, however, when the King was in occupation, the followers who were camping outside were surprised at night by Richard, Earl Marshall, who seized their horses and stores.

During the Glyndwr uprising the castle was attacked in March 1405 by a considerable Welsh force; however, it held out until assistance arrived. After the fifteenth century events bypassed Grosmont and neglect set in until the twentieth century.

Monmouth Castle, Monmouth NP5 3BS. Telephone: Monmouth (0600) 2935 or 2418. Cadw (viewing from exterior only).

Monmouth Castle stands on a hill which rises steeply from the banks of the river Monnow but there are few remains to be seen today. It was established by William Fitz Osbern in 1068 as one of the links in the defensive line from Clifford to Chepstow.

The most imposing part of the ruin is a massive rectangular two-storey block of the mid twelfth-century Great Tower containing the hall of the Norman castle. The upper storeys were built in 1340 and considerable alterations were made by the first Duke of Lancaster in the mid fifteenth century. It was the birthplace of Henry of Monmouth, who later became Henry V, on 9th August 1387.

In the Civil War the castle was surrendered on 19th August 1646 to the Parliamentarians, who destroyed the round tower in 1647. On 22nd December 1647 the bulk of the Great Tower fell down of its own accord, probably because of the collapse of tunnels dug beneath it in 1645.

Inside the castle grounds stands the handsome Great Castle House, which was built in 1673 by the third Marquis of Worcester (who later became the first Duke of Beaufort). It was built so that his daughter-in-law 'might lie in of her first child near the spot of Ground and Space of Air where our Great Hero, King Henry V was born'. It is in the renaissance style with a symmetrical facade and a flight of steps leading to the central doorway. Inside can be seen good examples of woodwork and ornate plaster ceilings. It is now occupied by the Royal Monmouthshire Royal Engineers (Militia) and free admission can be gained by prior appointment.

Penhow Castle, Penhow, near Newport. Telephone: Newport (0633) 400800.

Penhow Castle lies midway between Newport and Chepstow. It stands on a small hill which rises dramatically away from the main road. Roger de St Maur was in possession in 1129 when the stone tower was erected. It is a rectangular tower of three storeys with a projecting parapet. A Norman bedchamber has been restored within it.

The name St Maur gradually became anglicised to Seymour, and the castle remained in the family's possession until the late fourteenth century. In the fifteenth century castle passed by marriage to the Bowles family, and Sir Thomas Bowles remodelled the great hall with its screen and minstrel's gallery in about 1482. In the late seventeenth century the north range was refurbished with two fine panelled rooms and a baluster staircase, the medieval curtain wall being pierced with windows to make a classical facade overlooking the main road. The castle fell to use as a farm until 1966, and the present owner restored much of the building, setting it out with appropriate period furnishings. It is Wales's oldest inhabited castle and is open to the public.

18

Raglan Castle, Raglan. Telephone: Raglan (0291) 690228. Cadw.

It is not known if there was any military fortification at Raglan associated with the Norman conquest of Gwent. The present castle dates from the fifteenth century. Building there is believed to have commenced with Sir William ap Thomas, who was knighted by Henry VI and became Steward of the Lordships of Caerleon and Usk. It marks a transitional stage between a military fortification and a palatial residence in keeping with the growing wealth and power of the family. It stands on a rising piece of ground which drops away on the north-west side, where in its heyday formal gardens were laid out. Sir William built the Great Tower known as *Twr Melyn Gwent* (the 'yellow tower of Gwent', a name probably due to its covering of yellowish lichen) and probably the south gate and the south side of the hall. The Great Tower is a hexagonal five-storey building of great strength, surrounded by a deep water-filled moat. It is a self-contained fortified dwelling which could be held should the rest of the castle be lost.

Construction was continued by Sir William's son, William Herbert, Earl of Pembroke, who built the superb gatehouse block and added the residential apartments of the Fountain Court. He was succeeded by his son William and eventually the property passed by marriage to the Earls of Worcester. During the reign of Elizabeth I the hall and the domestic buildings in the Pitched Stone Court were renovated and the long gallery was added. At the end of this period niches were constructed in the moat walls, each filled with the statue of a Roman emperor.

During the Civil War Raglan Castle was the centre of the Royalist cause in south-west Britain. The Earl of Worcester was reputedly the richest man in Britain and loyal to the King. The garrison ignored a call to surrender in May 1646 but in June a considerable force of the New Model Army arrived to strengthen the siege. The east curtain wall was breached by cannon balls and the garrison finally capitulated on 19th August 1646 after ten weeks. Within a week of the surrender Parliament passed a resolution that the castle should be demolished, but apparently only breaches were blown in the outer walls. The paintings, statuary and books from the fine library all disappeared at this time.

Following the restoration of the monarchy the Worcesters were restored to their estates but the castle with its pleasure gardens and parkland was never again lived in by the family, who became the Dukes of Beaufort with their family seat at Badminton, now in Avon.

Skenfrith Castle, Skenfrith. National Trust/ Cadw (unlimited visiting). Telephone: Cardiff (0222) 465511.

It is probable that at the time when Chepstow and Monmouth castles were being built, earth and timber defences were established at Skenfrith. During the reign of Henry II (1154-89) Skenfrith was held by the Crown, being administered by the Sheriff of Herefordshire together with White Castle and Grosmont. Together these three castles largely controlled the area between Abergavenny and Monmouth and the three main east-west routes that pass through it. They remained in common ownership throughout the medieval period and became known as the Trilateral Castles.

The stone castle which survives today was built by Hubert de Burgh, who held Skenfrith for most of the time between 1201 and 1239. The round tower was the last part of the castle to be built and was probably not completed until 1244.

The castle consists of a rectangular enclosure with a drum tower at each corner. Originally the curtain walls were also protected by a moat on the south-west and north sides, of which nothing can be seen today. The river Monnow and the mill leat completed the water defences on the east side. Earth excavated from the moat was used to raise the

The Great Tower, Raglan Castle.

ground level inside the castle to create a mound on which the round tower was built, thus giving it additional height, so defenders could cover the curtain wall and shoot at the enemy outside.

The range of domestic buildings was along the western side of the curtain wall, where foundation walls can still be seen. A semi-circular tower was also added to the west wall to strengthen this part of the castle in the second half of the thirteenth century. It is solid up to the level of the wall walk.

White Castle, Llantilio Crossenny. Telephone: Llantilio (060 085) 380. Cadw.

White Castle stands on the summit of a commanding hill about a mile from Llantilio Crossenny. The earliest reference to it occurs in 1161-2, when it was referred to as 'Llantilio' after the manor in which it lies. As early as the thirteenth century, however, it is mentioned as White Castle, which refers to the white plaster which covered the masonry, fragments of which can still be seen.

In 1184 and 1186 £128 16s was spent on the castle, which probably paid for the construc-tion of the curtain wall enclosing the inner ward. The curtain wall in turn is protected by a moat. The original entrance to the castle was on the south-west side but the castle was re-orientated in the thirteenth century.

During the disturbances between Henry III and Simon de Montfort the Welsh under Llywelyn ap Gruffydd seized their opportunity to threaten the regime in the Welsh Marches and it was reported to the King in 1263 that the frontier held by Llywelyn was only a league and a half beyond Abergavenny. If Aber-gavenny fell, White Castle would be the next line of defence. It was at this time that White Castle was refortified. Strong circular flanking towers and a great gatehouse were added and an outer ward beyond the new gatehouse was enclosed by a stone wall, again protected by flanking towers.

The successful Edwardian conquest in North Wales deprived White Castle of its strategic function but it remained an administrative and financial centre of the manor. However, by the sixteenth century a survey shows that it was already roofless and derelict.

White Castle, Llantilio Crosseny.

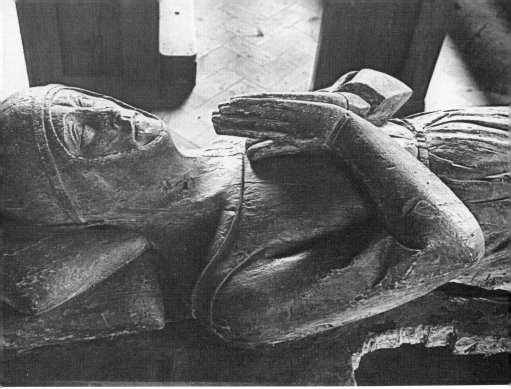

Wooden effigy in St Mary's church, Abergavenny.

5
Churches, chapels and monastic ruins

The earliest religion to exist in Britain was belief in special deities, nature worship, symbolism and druidism. When the Romans arrived they tried to destroy the power of the druids. Christianity came to Britain in the second century AD. It was not until AD 313 that the emperor Constantine officially tolerated Christianity. That it was not favoured by the Romans in authority in Gwent is evidenced by the martyrdom of Aaron and Julias at *Isca* (Caerleon) during the persecutions of Diocletian about AD 304.

When the Romans left Britain Gwent had become to a large extent Christian and by the time the Normans came to this area small churches and hermits' cells built of wood would have been in existence. After the conquest, churches were built in stone by Norman and native landowers and the Norman lords established monastic houses whose mother church was usually in France. The size of the church often depended on the wealth of the benefactor rather than on the population of the community.

The schism between the English church and Rome occurred in 1534 when Henry VIII became supreme head of the church in England and Wales and the dissolution of the monasteries followed. Gwent remained strongly Roman Catholic during the Commonwealth period and many wealthy families secretly maintained a priest and chapel. Following the Titus Oates plot a number of Roman Catholic priests who had been practising in Gwent were executed. One of them was Father David Lewis, who was born in Abergavenny, executed and buried at Usk (see chapter 8).

During the Commonwealth period, itinerant ministers were allowed to preach in Wales where there was most need. In 1646 Walter Cradock, Henry Walter and Richard Dymonds of Abergavenny were approved by the Assembly of Divines to be itinerant preachers. A division in the Independents over the question of baptism occurred and the Baptists broke away. A group was established in Abergavenny in 1652. The Quakers established a meeting house at Llanvihangel Ystern Llewern and the nonconformists broke away

21

following the Act of Uniformity in 1662. Methodism also took a strong hold in Wales during the eighteenth century and John Wesley visited Gwent in 1739.

Nonconformity and dissenting groups became especially influential and chapels became a dominant feature of the architecture of the South Wales valleys. Nonconformity emphasised the blessings of the world to come, compensating for the hard work and drab life of the ironworks and pit villages. Worldly amusements were unwelcome and Sundays were grimly pious. The strength of nonconformity lay in its comradeship, its readiness to face sacrifices and its strict morals, qualities which valley people still have today.

Monmouthshire ceased to be part of the diocese of Llandaff under the Welsh Church Act 1914 and in 1920 the Church in Wales became separate. In 1921 the new diocese of Monmouth was established with St Woolos, Newport, as the diocesan cathedral.

Abergavenny: St Mary.
St Mary's is sometimes called the 'Westminster Abbey of Wales' because it has a number of magnificent tombs. It was originally the church of the Benedictine priory established by Hamelin de Ballon before 1090 as a cell of the Abbey of St Vincent at Le Mans. Succeeding lords of Abergavenny were also benefactors. It appears to have been badly run and there was an enquiry into its administration as monks were said to be consorting with the women of the town and the prior Fulk Gaston absconded with the church silver. Following the dissolution of the monasteries, when it had only a prior and four monks, it became the parish church although it had been used by the townsfolk before this date.

The church is cruciform and impressively large, the chancel and nave being 172 feet (52 metres) in length. The central tower has eight bells. The church is mainly in the Decorated and Perpendicular styles and was refurbished in two phases in the nineteenth century. Little trace of Norman work survives. The oak choir stalls with misericords and carved lattice backs date from the fifteenth century and bear the name of the prior at that time — 'Wynchestre'. The prior's stall is raised and surmounted by a mitre.

The chief glory of the church is the effigies in wood, alabaster and marble dating from the thirteenth to the seventeenth centuries. There is a wooden figure of Jesse which once would have formed part of a 'Jesse tree' showing the ancestry of Jesus. Another wooden effigy, in the nave, is probably that of John de Hastings, Lord of Abergavenny. It is of a young knight wearing a long surcoat over a hauberk and hood of chain mail.

In the Lewis Chapel there are two female effigies. One holds a heart (probably indicating a 'heart only' burial dating from the end of the thirteenth century) and, although her identity is unknown, she must have been an important lady as she is covered with a shield bearing a coat of arms, which is unusual for a woman. The other effigy dates from the fourteenth century and is said to be Eva de Broase, who died by falling from the castle walls when chasing her pet squirrel. The chain from her waist was once attached to a squirrel but as with many tombs the carving was defaced during the Commonwealth.

The Herbert Chapel contains recumbent monuments of the Hastings and Herbert families in alabaster and marble. There are also a number of interesting brasses from the sixteenth and seventeenth centuries. The Norman font was rediscovered in the churchyard during the nineteenth century: it had been turned out of the church by a Baptist minister, John Abbot, who did not believe in infant baptism, during the seventeenth century.

Bettws Newydd
A chapelry was founded here by Aeddan in the thirteenth century. This small church contains the most complete rood loft and screen in Wales. It dates from the fifteenth century and is thoroughly Welsh in character. It is carved with bulbous vine leaves, which look more like oak leaves but which bear grapes and tendrils. There is no chancel arch so the timbering is continued right up to the roof. Apart from this outstanding piece of craftsmanship, the church is plain. The font is Norman and decorated with cable moulding.

Blaenavon: St Peter.
The building of this church in 1805 was financed by the proprietors of the Blaenavon Ironworks. It reflects the craft skills of the workers in the town: pillars, window frames, door sills, tomb covers and even the font are all made in iron. Inside there are memorials to those members of the Hopkins and Hill families who were buried in Blaenavon. In the churchyard there are examples of tombs made in iron.

Chepstow: St Mary.
St Mary's church was part of the Benedictine priory founded by William Fitz Osbern in the eleventh century as a daughter to the abbey of Cormeilles in France. It became the parish church at the Dissolution. None of the priory buildings survives. The church retains a Norman doorway on the west side. A deeply recessed arch is carried on five pillars on either side of the door with zigzag carving decorating the arches, with two secondary arches on either side of the entrance.

The tower collapsed in the early eighteenth

century and in 1841 an almost complete rebuilding took place, followed by restoration in 1890 in an attempt to remedy some of the earlier alterations. The church now consists of chancel, broad transepts and a nave of six bays. Five of the bays are original and have massive square piers. The former groined ceiling was replaced by a handsomely decorated flat ceiling of oak.

There are a number of interesting memorials in the church. One to Henry Marten (see chapter 8) has an epitaph which he composed himself, with the first letter of each line reading downwards to form his name. The other two imposing tombs are those of Henry Somerset, second Earl of Worcester (died 1549), and his wife, Elizabeth, and of Margaret Clayton with her two husbands, Thomas Shipman and Richard Clayton, kneeling in attitudes of prayer above her recumbent form. These two tombs have been repainted by the local artist Keith Underwood as they might have originally been decorated.

Cwmfelinfach: Islwyn Memorial (Babell) Chapel, Islwyn Street, Cwmfelinfach, near Risca. Telephone: Cross Keys (0495) 200434 or Cwmbran (063 33) 67711 extension 665.

The Babell Chapel was built in 1827 for a Calvinistic-Methodist congregation. It is a small building, typical of the valley chapels, whitewashed on the outside. The most famous preacher who ministered there was Daniel Jenkins, brother-in-law of the Reverend William Thomas (1832-78). Thomas is better known by his bardic title 'Islwyn' and famed for his poetry. There is a monument to him in the tiny walled graveyard. The chapel still has its original simple furnishings and pulpit but it ceased to be used for religious services in the 1960s. It is now a visitor centre.

Cwmyoy: St Martin.

Cwmyoy church stands on the steep hillside of the Honddu valley. The valley side is subject to landslips and subsidence, which have severely affected the church perched on the slopes. It stands below a spur of the hillside and over the centuries its walls and tower have gradually moved with the slipping hillside. The tower now stands at what seems to be a perilous angle and the whole body of the church is twisted. To prevent further movement the whole church is stoutly buttressed.

The tower houses six bells, although for safety reasons only two are rung. Inside the church stands a medieval cross which was discovered in 1871 at a nearby farm. It is thought to be one of the crosses on the Pilgrim Way to St David's. In 1967 it was stolen from the church but luckily recovered by a Keeper of Sculpture at the British Museum from a

Babell chapel, Cwmfelinfach, where the poet 'Islwyn' is buried.

London antique dealer's shop. He identified it as dating from the thirteenth century. An unusual feature is that the figure of Christ on the cross is carved wearing a mitre.

Llangwm: St Heirom or St Jerome.

The glory of Llangwm church is the ornately carved rood screen and rood loft which date from the early sixteenth century. They are very delicately carved with vine leaves and tracery which give them a lace-like quality. The church dates from the thirteenth century and has a large square tower built in the seventeenth century, with a pentagonal projecting stair turret.

In the churchyard one gravestone records a local murder, that of Elizabeth Gwin of The Poulth who was murdered in her own house on 28th June 1743 aged 84 years:

'Here lieth the body that lost its life
By bloody villain full of strife
Who coveted boath gold and land
As anybody may understand...'

Although his grave is not marked, this church is also the burial site of Walter Cradock, an ejected clergyman who became a prominent Independent preacher.

Llangwm was given to the see of Llandaff by Cynfelyn about AD 700. In 1128 a papal bull mentions the village of Llangwm 'with its churches', which confirms the ancient foundation of the church at Llangwm Isaf which stands about 600 yards (550 metres) away.

Llanthony Priory

The name Llanthony is a corruption of Llandewi Nant Honddu — 'the church of St David on the Honddu brook'. Towards the end of the reign of William II a knight called William de Lacy, kinsman to Hugh de Lacy, Lord of Ewyas, tired after a long day's hunt, became separated from his companions and rested beside the ruined cell in this beautiful valley 'truly fitted for contemplation'. The serenity of the surroundings here caused him to renounce the pleasures of the world and become a hermit. He was joined by Ernisius, chaplain to Queen Matilda, and they rebuilt the chapel. They received endowments from Hugh de Lacy and founded a monastery for Black Canons of the Order of St Augustine. During the term of the third prior the valley became the centre of warfare between Welsh tribes and the monks fled to Hereford. The Earl of Hereford granted them some land near Gloucester, where they founded another house, also called Llanthony Priory, in 1136-7.

Towards the end of the twelfth century the de Lacy family made large grants to Llanthony and this heralded a new phase of building. It was dissolved in 1536 when its revenues amounted to just under £100.

Although now in ruins, the buildings are still magnificent. The church is 252 feet (77 metres) long and 50 feet (15 metres) wide and had a central tower 100 feet (30 metres) high (the upper portion has now gone). The aisleless

St Martin's church, Cwmyoy.

24

Llanthony Priory.

choir, which is plain and severe, appears to have been the earliest work. The western front, with its twin towers in three stages, is in good condition. A magnificent window between the towers was intact until 1803, when it collapsed. The south tower and the prior's dwelling have been converted into the Abbey Hotel. The bar, which serves real ales, is in vaulted rooms below ground level. Court Farm is also built into the ruins of the priory. The hospitium was probably built between 1180 and 1220 and is now the little parish church.

Llanthony is a place of extraordinary beauty and has attracted a number of famous people including Walter Savage Landor, Father Ignatius (see chapter 8) and Eric Gill, sculptor, wood-carver and designer of fine type-faces such as 'Perpetua' and 'Gill Sans'.

Llanvair Kilgeddin: St Mary.
St Mary's is a little church of ancient foundation standing in a bend of the river Usk. It was sensitively rebuilt in 1876 by the architect J. D. Sedding, but its fame lies in its decorated interior. The whole is decorated with sgraffito work carried out by Heywood Sumner in 1888-90. Sgraffito is a technique consisting of applying three coats of plaster with different colours to a wall and then cutting a design to reveal the colours below. The work was commissioned by the vicar, the Reverend William John Coussmaker Lindsay, in memory of his wife, Rosamund Emily, who died in 1885. The scenes illustrate the Benedicite, and Sumner used the local landscape for the 'mountains and hills'. The Blorenge, Sugar Loaf and Skirrid together with the river Usk and the tower of nearby Llanfihangel Gobion church appear in the scenes.

Newport: Cathedral Church of St Woolos.
The church of St Woolos, formerly the parish church of Newport, was created the cathedral church of the diocese of Monmouth in 1921. It stands in a commanding position on Stow Hill and its exterior appearance gives no indication of the wealth of Norman architecture inside.

The church follows the slope of the ground, so the nave is two steps lower than the west end of the church. The lower parts of the western tower were probably built by Humphrey, sixth Earl of Stafford, in the early

25

Mural at Llanvair Kilgeddin church, depicting the Blorenge, Sugar Loaf and Skirrid mountains.

fifteenth century and completed later in the century. In a niche on the west side is a decapitated effigy in stone wearing the badge of a Knight of the Garter; it is said to be either Jasper Tudor or Humphrey Stafford.

The western part of the church dates from the thirteenth century and is said to be the site of the cell of St Gwynllyw (or Woolos), to whom the church is dedicated. The late Norman doorway leading to the nave is the great architectural feature of the cathedral. It is composed of four richly carved concentric bands resting on two columns. The nave is also late Norman with all but one of the five bays having zigzag moulding on the arches.

There are a number of fine monuments, including one to Sir John Morgan and his wife, an imposing Jacobean tomb of Sir Walter Herbert of St Julians and a memorial to Benjamin Pratt, founding partner in the Blaenavon Ironworks.

Skenfrith: St Bridget or St Bride.

The thirteenth-century church stands over-looking the river Monnow. The low but massive west tower, strongly buttressed and with small narrow lancets, is topped with a

picturesque wooden belfry with a lantern roof, an unusual feature in this county. It has six bells, which are all dated 1764.

Inside, an arcade of four bays separates the nave from the north aisle, which was probably built in the fourteenth century. The south aisle is later still. Little is left of the original chancel. In the east window can be seen a few fragments of ancient glass. Beneath the communion table is a pre-Reformation altar slab.

In the north aisle is a handsome medieval cope dating from about 1500. It is made of red velvet, richly embroidered with the Virgin Mary and Jesus below a trefoil canopy stitched on the hood. Below this are embroidered three angels and two double-headed eagles encircling the scene of the Assumption of the Virgin. It is enriched with elegant floral designs.

There are two square family pews, one of them belonging to the Morgan family, and an altar tomb of John ap Philip Morgan (died 1557) and his wife, Anne. The octagonal font dates from 1661, and the same date is marked on the roof timbers.

Tintern Abbey

Tintern is famed not only for its abbey but

26

also for the beauty of its natural setting on the banks of the river Wye. Tintern Abbey was established in 1131 by Walter de Clare, Lord of Chepstow, for monks of the Cistercian order in a place away from the turmoil and corruption of town life.

The original Norman buildings were rebuilt in the thirteenth century and the church was completely rebuilt between 1270 and 1301 by Roger Bigod, who inherited the lordship of Chepstow. It is built in the Decorated style and, although now lacking a roof (the roof lead was melted down to raise money for the Tudor dynasty), is remarkably complete. The frame of the great seven-light west window, which is 42 feet (13 metres) high, is still intact and when filled with decorated glass must have been a stunning sight. The church is 228 feet (69 metres) long by 150 feet (46 metres) wide. The east window is even larger than the west, being 64 feet (20 metres) high. It now frames views of the steeply wooded hill slopes of the Wye valley.

Beside the church are the remains of the other monastic buildings. To the north lies the cloister, surrounded by the chapter house, library and vestry on one side and the novices' lodgings with the monks' dormitory above, the monks' dining hall, the kitchen and the lay brothers' dining hall on the other side. Other major buildings include the infirmary with its own cloister and the abbot's hall.

It was from a position overlooking the abbey that Wordsworth wrote his poem 'Lines Written above Tintern Abbey' but it appears that the beauty of the scene below him defied description because he later wrote:

'To those who know not no words can paint

And those who know thee know all words are feint.'

Trelleck: St Nicholas.

This is one of the many churches in the county which appears to be too large for the community it serves. The present building dates from the fourteenth century and has an impressive 180 foot (55 metre) spire rising above an embattled tower.

Inside, the fine Early English nave is lit by trefoil lancets and larger windows dating from the fourteenth and fifteenth centuries. The church contains some interesting woodwork. The panelled pulpit dated 1640 was once part of a three-decker pulpit and the oak sanctuary rails are formed of barley-sugar twists. Note also the inner doors, which bear on the inside the date 1595 together with the sacred monogram, both in inlaid lead. It also houses the

carved arms of Charles II, presented in 1683 because the village supported the Royalist cause. They were repainted in 1977 to celebrate the Silver Jubilee of Elizabeth II. There is also an interesting sundial (see chapter 10) and three fonts, one of which was found acting as a base to the sundial.

Outside is a preaching cross probably dating from the eighth century. It is believed to have once stood in Cross Lane, where a base still stands. Beside it is a massive stone altar composed of a slab 8 feet (2.4 metres) long, 3 feet (0.9 metre) wide and 1 foot (0.3 metre) thick. Its supports are carved with Celtic crosses in circles.

Usk: St Mary.

Originally this was the church of the Benedictine priory for nuns founded by Richard de Clare before his death in 1135. The nave and the north aisle formed the parish church of the town. The central tower separated the monastic and parochial sections and the tower was spared when the chancel and transepts of the convent were destroyed.

The four arches of the former crossing are original work dating from the first quarter of the twelfth century, as is the massive tower above it, though the tower has had later embellishments. The nave is in the Decorated style with Perpendicular additions. The north aisle was added in the thirteenth century but rebuilt and widened in the fifteenth century, when the elaborate north and west porches were also added.

The church has a finely worked rood screen dating from the fifteenth century and probably of Gloucestershire or Somerset workmanship. An unusual feature of the church is the circular stair turret which projects into the aisle and ascends the north-west angle of the tower.

Inside the church is a brass plate inscribed in medieval Welsh which commemorates the chronicler Adam of Usk (see chapter 8). It is the earliest known example of a brass inscription in the Welsh language. In the south wall of the nave is to be found the impressive monument of Roger Edwards of Allt-y-bela (a magnificent but sadly neglected house outside Usk) who founded the grammar school in the town and endowed almshouses at Llangeview.

Outside the door is the supposed grave of St David Lewis (see chapter 8), who was executed in Usk in 1678 for adhering to the Roman Catholic faith. Most of the other convent buildings have disappeared although fragments are incorporated in the house known as Usk Priory.

Big Pit Mining Museum.

6
Museums and historic houses

ABERGAVENNY
Abergavenny Museum, The Castle, Castle Street, Abergavenny NP7 5EE. Telephone: Abergavenny (0873) 4282.

Abergavenny Museum is situated in the grounds of the ruins of Abergavenny Castle in a house and the adjoining 'keep' built in 1819. It is a local history museum with permanent displays showing a Welsh farmhouse kitchen of about 1900, a saddler's workshop and a governess cart made by Samuel Probert of Abergavenny. It also has a seventeenth-century mural of the Adoration of the Magi which is thought to be the reredos of an altar found in the secret chapel of the Gunter family's mansion in Cross Street. It was there that Father David Lewis held services for Roman Catholics (see chapter 8). Changing temporary exhibitions show other aspects of the local history of the area, using the museum's collections of photographs, prints, ephemera, agricultural and craft tools.

BLAENAVON
Big Pit Mining Museum, Big Pit, Blaenavon NP4 9XP. Telephone: Blaenavon (0495) 790311.

This was a working coal mine until 1980, when it closed down and became a museum of mining. It had been worked for coal for over a hundred years. Visitors, equipped with safety helmet, miner's lamp and battery, can descend 300 feet (90 metres) underground in a cage. Former miners who used to work in the pit act as guides to the underground workings, where different techniques of coal extraction can be seen. The underground stables for the pit ponies are also visited. On the surface there is a blacksmith's forge, the interior of a miner's cottage, a winding engine house, the pithead baths and an audio-visual display about the history of the pit.

CAERLEON
Roman Legionary Museum, High Street, Caerleon NP6 1AE. Telephone: Newport (0633) 423134.

The Roman Legionary Museum is housed in purpose-built premises which retain the classical portico of the original museum built in 1850. The display includes excavated material from the legionary fortress at Usk which was abandoned in favour of the site at Caerleon. The museum illustrates the life and history of the Second Augustan Legion, which garrisoned the fortress at Caerleon, and of the civil settlements which grew up around it (including Great Bulmore). One of the most exciting finds which can be seen is a copper strigil (scraper) which was found in the drain of the Fortress Baths. It is inlaid in silver, gold and brass with scenes from the labours of Hercules. A remarkable collection of 88 engraved gemstones also came from the drain.

CALDICOT
Caldicot Castle Museum, The Castle, Caldicot NP6 4HU. Telephone: Caldicot (0291) 420241.

The various parts of the castle house museum displays. In the Gatehouse are displays relating to the castle, with a costume exhibition on the first floor. In other towers are to be found displays on the history of the town, the castle and its owners and period rooms. The three-storey Woodstock Tower acts as an art gallery for temporary exhibitions. An unexpected item to be found in the castle is the figurehead of the *Foudroyant*, Lord Nelson's flagship, which was purchased in 1892 by J. R. Cobb, who renovated the castle in the late nineteenth century. He restored the ship at the cost of £30,000 but it was wrecked in a gale at Blackpool in 1897.

CHEPSTOW
Chepstow Museum, Gwy House, Bridge Street, Chepstow NP6 5EZ. Telephone: Chepstow (029 12) 5981.

Chepstow Museum occupies a fine eighteenth-century town house built by a wealthy Chepstow merchant who was also an apothecary by profession. In the twentieth century Gwy House has been used as a school and as a

hospital. It is now a local history museum with displays showing the development of the town as an important port trading predominantly in wine, timber and oak bark. There are displays on shipbuilding, salmon fishing and other local industries, together with photographs and ephemera showing the entertainments and social life of the town. A good collection of topographical prints and watercolours of Chepstow and the Wye Valley shows that the area has long attracted both artists and tourists. The museum also has a programme of varied temporary exhibitions.

CWMBRAN
Llanyrafon Farm, Llanfrechfa Way, Cwmbran NP4 6HT. Torfaen Museum Trust. Telephone: Pontypool (049 55) 52036.

Llanyrafon was the chief estate and manor house of the parish of Llanfrechfa until the late nineteenth century. From the early seventeenth century to 1886 it was owned by the Griffith family, and the house reflects the growth in the family's wealth and social status. It is being developed as a museum of rural history and from 1988 there will be a number of period room displays showing the changing phases of the house and also outbuildings illustrating a typical late Victorian valley farm with livestock and farm gardens.

LLANVIHANGEL CRUCORNEY
Llanvihangel Court, Llanvihangel Crucorney, near Abergavenny. Telephone: Abergavenny (0873) 890217.

The present house is Tudor in appearance

Governess cart made by Samuel Probert, in Abergavenny Museum, with 'Cockle' in harness.

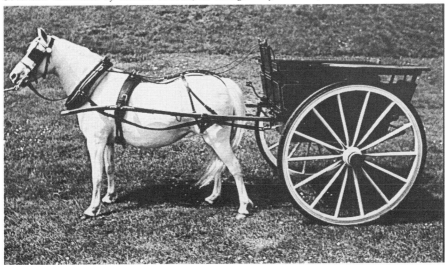

29

but has developed from a medieval hall house with domestic rooms on one side and the private family apartments on the other. The front of the east wing was rebuilt in 1559 by Rhys Morgan. In 1627 it was purchased by Nicholas Arnold, who was member of Parliament for Monmouthshire in 1626. His grandson was well known for breeding horses and the seventeenth-century stables at the rear of the house are ascribed to him. The rooms are furnished with pieces of various periods. Notable items include a painting of the house and grounds in about 1680 with the Skirrid Fawr in the background, a magnificent staircase in yew and a fine moulded plaster ceiling patterned with intertwined hearts amongst Tudor roses and fleurs-de-lys.

MONMOUTH
Nelson Museum and Local History Centre, Priory Street, Monmouth NP5 3XA. Telephone: Monmouth (0600) 3519.

The Nelson Museum has an important collection of national significance relating to Horatio Nelson. It was started by Lady Llangattock, who began collecting Nelson memorabilia towards the end of the nineteenth century. She later presented it to the town. Nelson's fighting sword and letters to his wife and Lady Hamilton are among the personal items on display, together with commemora-

Part of a poster of 1806, at the Nelson Museum and Local History Centre, Monmouth.

BRITONS !
Your NELSON is dead!
Trust not in an Arm of Flesh, but in the *Living* GOD!
WHAT SAID THE BRAVE
Nelson, Duncan, Howe?
" GOD hath given us the VICTORY !"
His Arm is not cold in Death, nor shortened that it cannot Save.
BRITONS!
Fear GOD, Fear SIN, And Then
Fear Nothing.

tive pottery, silver, glass, prints, paintings and models. Amongst the fake Nelson mementoes is his supposed glass eye (although he probably could not see, he never actually lost his eye and the object is a surgeon's teaching model).

The Local History Centre has displays dealing with the development of Monmouth from a Norman fortress and settlements to a bustling market town. The museum also houses the borough archive and personal documents and old photographs relating to Charles Rolls (see chapter 8) and his family. Temporary exhibitions show other aspects of the town. The museum shares a building with the post office designed by George Maddox in 1834. In 1963 it was completely gutted by fire and everything behind the street facade was rebuilt.

NEWPORT
Newport Museum and Art Gallery, 5 John Frost Square, Newport NP9 1HZ. Telephone: Newport (0633) 840064.

The museum was founded in 1888 in Lower Dock Street and moved to its present purpose-built premises in 1968. The museum is located on the first floor and the art gallery on the third floor. The archaeology displays include Roman material excavated from *Venta Silurum* (Caerwent), ranging from ornaments, tools and household utensils to painted wall plaster, sculpture and a splendid mosaic representing the four seasons. An exhibition called 'The Making of Newport' illustrates the local and social history of the town. The natural history section features the plant and animal life of Gwent with local habitats displaying rocks, fossils, insects and birds.

The large art gallery has a varied programme of temporary exhibitions. The permanent collections include a major collection of English watercolours of the eighteenth and nineteenth centuries with local prints and drawings. It also has a growing collection of Welsh paintings, modern ceramics and prints.

Tredegar House and Country Park, Coedkernew, Newport NP1 9YW. Telephone: Newport (0633) 62275. Newport Borough Council.

Tredegar House is located 2 miles (3 km) west of Newport (leave the M4 motorway at junction 28). For over 500 years it was the ancestral home of the Morgans, lords of Tredegar. Parts of a stone-built medieval house remain, but extensive rebuilding in brick took place in the late seventeenth century, making Tredegar House the finest country house in South Wales. Following substantial restoration, over forty rooms are open to the public, each decorated and furnished for a particular period. The guided tour takes in not only the lavish oak carvings of the Brown Room and the splendid stucco and gold-leaf decoration of the Gilt Room but also the great

Tredegar House, near Newport.

kitchens and servants' quarters 'below stairs'.

The house is surrounded by 90 acres (36 ha) of parkland, lake and gardens, as well as a fine range of estate outbuildings (the stable block is particularly impressive), some of which are now used as craft workshops and visitor facilities.

PONTYPOOL

Junction Cottage, Lower Mill, Pontymoel, Pontypool. Torfaen Museum Trust. Telephone: Pontypool (049 55) 52036.

This is a canal keeper's cottage, built in 1814, situated on a lock at the junction of the Brecon and Abergavenny Canal and the Monmouthshire Canal. Inside are exhibitions about the canal and the people who lived in the cottage, including a furnished room.

The Valley Inheritance, Pontypool, Park Buildings, Pontypool NP4 6JH. Torfaen Museum Trust. Telephone: Pontypool (049 55) 52036.

The Valley Inheritance, Pontypool, is housed in the former stable block, built about 1830, of Pontypool Park House. It is a gracious building whose external appearance reflects its original function. Inside modern exhibitions tell the story, through original objects, photographs and film, of the eastern industrial valley of Gwent, which was the birthplace of important technological innovations. Displays tell the story of the valley from earliest times to the present day, placing emphasis on the changes which took place after 1780.

RISCA

Risca Industrial History Museum, Oxford House, Risca NP1 6GN. Telephone: Risca (0633) 612245.

This museum has displays of industrial archaeology and a reconstruction of a chemist's shop from Edwardian times. It is open only on Saturday mornings.

USK

Gwent Rural Life Museum, The Malt Barn, New Market Street, Usk NP5 1AU. Telephone: Usk (029 13) 3777 or Tredunnock (063 349) 315.

This award-winning museum was started by a local farmer in Llanvapley who saw how rapidly the agricural way of life was changing. It is now run by volunteers and is housed in a building which may have originated as a merchant's dwelling in the fifteenth century but more recently was used as a storage barn for the maltster's house next door. Inside are displays of a farmhouse kitchen, farm wagons, tractors, craft tools, vintage machinery, a laundry and a dairy.

WOLVESNEWTON

Wolvesnewton Model Farm, Folk and Craft Centre, Wolvesnewton, near Chepstow. Telephone: Wolvesnewton (029 15) 231.

The model farm is located just off the B4235 at Llangwm, 4 miles (6 km) from Usk and 10 miles (16 km) from Chepstow. It was built at the end of the eighteenth century for the Duke of Beaufort and is in the form of a unique cross-shaped barn. The folk collection covers domestic and agricultural life since the beginning of the nineteenth century with a light-hearted look at everyday life and the robust humour of days gone by. In the adjacent mill there are temporary exhibitions of art or photography. In the series of workshops you can watch craftsmen and women at work making pottery, corn-dollies, jewellery and woodwork, and their products can be bought.

Blaenavon Ironworks in 1800 by Sir Richard Colt Hoare.

Forge Row at Cwmavon.

7
Industrial history

Iron was made in Gwent before the Romans arrived. It is recorded in such names as *Gobannium* for Roman Abergavenny. Gobannius was the god of the ironsmith, hence 'the place of the ironsmiths'. The south-western part of the county and the Wye valley had the mineral resources as well as timber for smelting.

In the late fifteenth century the blast furnace was introduced to Britain. By harnessing water power to work mechanical bellows which created higher temperatures, iron output could be greatly increased. Early furnaces are usually found on the banks of rivers in wooded areas. There is evidence of early ironmaking at Monmouth, Raglan, Tintern, Brynmawr and Pontypool.

For many years men had been trying to use coal instead of charcoal to smelt the iron ore but the impurities in the coal made the iron brittle and useless. About 1709 Abraham Darby of Coalbrookdale, Shropshire, discovered that if coal was burnt to form coke good-quality iron could be obtained. Even better results were obtained if limestone was added as a flux. Gwent had all the necessary resources in abundance and this soon led to the industrialisation of the western part of the county.

As well as the industrial site there are also the remains to be seen of the superstructure which develops with industry — housing for the workers and ironmasters, communications in the form of tramroads, canals and railways and evidence of winning the minerals in the form of pits and quarries. Many of the sites are on privately owned land but can be explored by following footpaths, such as in the Clydach Valley. Great care should be taken by visitors and particularly by parents with children, as many of the sites have been abandoned for a number of years and no attempt has been made to make them safe for visitors. The following sites are just a few of the best examples in the county. For each site the National Grid map reference is given together with the Ordnance Survey 1:50,000 map sheet number.

Blaenavon Ironworks, Blaenavon (OS 161, SO 251095). Telephone: Cardiff (0222) 465511. Cadw.

Blaenavon Ironworks is the best surviving example of a late eighteenth-century ironworks in Britain. The first ironworks at Blaenavon, started in the 1780s, consists of a bank of blast furnaces set into the hillside. This arrangement enabled the furnaces to be filled

33

from the upper level and then after blasting the molten metal could be run off from the bottom into the casting houses, where it was moulded into bars or 'pigs'.

When Coxe visited Blaenavon in 1800 he described the works: 'At some distance, the works have the appearance of a small town, surrounded with heaps of ore, coal and limestone, and enlivened with the bustle and activity of an opulent and increasing establishment. The view of the buildings, which are constructed in the excavations of the rocks, is extremely picturesque, and heightened by the volumes of black smoke emitted by the furnaces.'

Production reached a peak in the 1820s and after this investment was made to modernise the works. A large stone balance tower, which dominates the site, was built in the 1830s to ease the moving of goods from one level to another, using water as a counterweight to the cargo. By the late nineteenth century the works were obsolete, having been replaced by a new plant on the other side of the valley at Forgeside.

The Brecon and Abergavenny Canal

An Act of Parliament was passed in 1792 allowing for the construction of the canal. It was surveyed by Thomas Dadford junior and work began in 1794 with the construction of an embankment and aqueduct over the river Clydach. It reached Brecon in 1800 and the 33 miles (53 km) southwards to Pontymoel (where it joined the Monmouthshire Canal) were completed in 1812 at the cost of £200,000. At first its trade was largely agricultural, consisting of lime, manure and farm produce, together with coal to Brecon, but when it was joined to the Monmouthshire Canal it could carry industrial products to Newport docks.

In the beginning it had three associated tramroads, Beaufort to Gilwern, Gilwern to Glangrwyney and Llanfoist to Abergavenny. Wharves can be seen at Llanfoist and Gilwern. The last toll on the canal was collected in 1933. The canal between Pontymoel and Brecon is now re-opened to navigation. It is used for pleasure cruising and the towpath as a long-distance footpath.

The Clydach Valley

The gorge is 3½ miles (6 km) long and less than ½ mile (800 metres) wide and descends from Brynmawr at 1100 feet (338 metres) to 400 feet (122 metres) above sea level near Abergavenny. It contains a number of sites: rocky amphitheatres left by quarrying, massive stone arches, chapels, humble terraces and a tracery of transport systems etched into the valley sides.

Llanelly Furnace (OS 161, SO 232138) and forge were established in the seventeenth century by the Hanbury family of Pontypool. The 'Clerk to the Furnace' lived in the fine seventeenth-century Clydach House. Francis Lewis put his coat of arms above the main entrance with the date 1693. The furnace was in production in 1684 but was superseded by the **Clydach Ironworks** (OS 161, SO 229132), using coke, established before 1795. It remained in production for about 65 years. By 1841 over 1350 people were employed, including small children, occupied in digging ore and coal. The remains of the blast furnaces can still be seen.

Llanelly Quarry (OS 161, SO 222124) originally supplied the Clydach Ironworks with limestone but it also burnt lime for agricultural purposes and supplied stone for road building. A double limekiln stands near the entrance and a second pair inscribed 1892 stands near the standard-gauge railway. The quarry was closed in the mid 1930s.

Clydach Limeworks (OS 161, SO 233127) stands near the railway viaduct, which was widened to two tracks in 1877 (the date the kilns were constructed). Remains of the tramroads constructed by the Baileys can also be seen. The limekilns are fine examples with a double draw arch for each shaft. An older pair stands near the stream, Nant Dyar, and has single arches. Tramroads lead down the valley to a wharf on the Brecon and Abergavenny Canal. The stone blocks which carried the rails can be seen in the woods alongside the river Clydach.

There are a number of trails leading walkers around the sites in the valley.

Crumlin Viaduct site, Crumlin (OS 171, ST 213985).

Here stood the most famous viaduct in South Wales. It was said to be the largest railway bridge in the world composed wholly of iron. It spanned the Ebbw valley at a height of 210 feet (64 metres) carrying the Taff Vale extension of the Newport, Abergavenny and Hereford Railway. It was started in 1853, the foundation stone being laid by Lady Isabella Fitzmaurice. It was demolished in 1966.

Cwmbyrgwm Water Balance Pit, Abersychan (OS 171, SO 251033).

This is the last water-balance winding gear in South Wales still remaining in its original position. In the first half of the nineteenth century there were more than sixty of these in operation in Gwent.

Ebbw Vale Iron and Steel Works, Ebbw Vale (OS 161, SO 172085).

A coke-fired blast furnace was established here in 1790. In 1868 the works were converted to steel production but could not survive the depression in the iron and steel industry and the fall in coal prices in the late 1920s. To provide jobs in an area of high unemployment the government intervened and a new steelworks was begun in 1936 and went into production in 1938. Iron and steel production ceased in 1978 and the works is now used only for galvanising and tinplate manufacture.

Forge Row, Cwmavon (OS 161, SO 270064). Torfaen Museum Trust. Telephone: Pontypool (049 55) 52036.

Forge Row was built in 1804 for workers at the Varteg Forge (which no longer exists) on the opposite side of the modern road. It was far ahead of its time in that the row was better constructed and had a larger floor area than was usual and even had roof insulation. The houses of Forge Row were the first industrial cottages in South Wales to have back doors. The row has changed little from its original design and appearance.

The Monmouthshire Canal and Fourteen Locks Canal Centre, (OS 171; ST 280886), High Cross, Rogerstone, near Newport. Telephone: Newport (0633) 894802 or Cwmbran (063 33) 67711 extension 665.

The Monmouthshire Canal was constructed from Newport to Pontymoel (11 miles, 18 km) with a branch to Crumlin (12 miles, 19 km) which left the main line at Malpas. The canal and tramroads were declared open in 1799. In 1853, to prevent competition for the growing railway network, the company became the Monmouthshire Railway and Canal Company and a year later the canal was cut short to improve the railway connections to the docks and wharves in Newport. In 1880 it was taken over by the Great Western Railway. The Crumlin branch was closed in 1949. Parts of it have now been taken over for roads and other purposes and portions are derelict, while other areas have been restored. This includes the area round Fourteen Locks near Rogerstone.

The Crumlin branch rises 358 feet (109 metres) through 32 locks, fourteen of which are within a ½ mile (800 metre) stretch. These were controlled by a complicated system of ponds, channels, tunnels and weirs which enabled barges to be raised or lowered 168 feet (51 metres) with a minimum of water wastage from the canal.

The exhibition in the Canal Centre traces the growth and decline of the canals in Gwent. The last cargo boat went through Fourteen Locks in 1930.

Sirhowy Ironworks, Sirhowy (OS 161, SO 143102).

At Sirhowy are the remains of the first coke-fired blast furnace to be established in Gwent (1778). By 1840 there were four furnaces producing 7000 tons of iron annually. The works closed in 1883 in the face of competition from more modern plant. In 1805 the Sirhowy tramroad was completed, linking the Sirhowy and Tredegar Ironworks with Newport. Until 1829 the trams were horse-drawn but then a steam locomotive hauled the first load of 57 tons of iron at 6 mph (10 km/h), which was twice the speed of horses.

Stack Square and Engine Row, Blaenavon. Adjacent to Blaenavon Ironworks (OS 161; SO 251095).

These were originally part of one of the earliest industrial settlements built in Wales. Other dwellings were demolished in the 1960s and 1970s. The two parallel rows of houses are joined by a third range of buildings which in the early nineteenth century contained the company shop, works offices and a first-floor dormitory for labourers. The whole group was built between 1788 and 1792.

The houses have two rooms on each floor and a larder. By the standards of their time they are quite large, which suggests they were built for the foreman and craftsmen many of whom were from the Midlands, where iron-making technology was at its most advanced.

Sudbrook (OS 171; ST 50784).

When the Severn Tunnel was being constructed by Thomas Walker from 1880 this small village was built to house the workers and provide them with a school, hospital, mission hall, infirmary and a coffee tavern, but no pub.

In 1883 the tunnel was flooded when excavations broke into an underground spring. To deal with this problem, Walker built the pumping station and used Cornish beam engines to lower the level of the water. This is now done electrically and the beam engines are no longer there. 24 million gallons (109 million litres) of water are extracted on an average day. The 4 mile (6 km) tunnel was completed in 1886 and the first passenger train went through on 1st December.

Tintern Abbey Furnace, Tintern (OS 162, SO 514003).

In 1500-50 a wireworks was established at Tintern in the Angidy valley, where fast-running water could power the machinery. It was the first in Britain to use water power rather than man power in the wire-drawing process; about 1600 a furnace was established to supply the wireworks with iron.

35

The Bevan Memorial Stones, near Tredegar.

8
Famous people

Gwent seems to hold a particular attraction for writers, poets and artists, **William Makepeace Thackeray** visited in 1842 and remarked on the cheapness of his board and lodgings in Chepstow, the beauty of the surroundings and 'in the Wye the best salmon that was ever eaten in the world'. **Alfred, Lord Tennyson,** the Poet Laureate, stayed at the Hanbury Arms in Caerleon to gain inspiration for his *Idylls of the King.* On 16th September 1856 he wrote: 'The Usk murmurs by the window and I sit like King Arthur in Caerleon.' **William Wordsworth** wrote 'Lines Written above Tintern Abbey', on revisiting the Wye valley in 1798:
> 'O sylvan Wye! Thou wanderer thro'
> the woods,
> How often had my spirit turned to
> thee!'

J. M. W. Turner travelled through Gwent on two occasions, painting local scenes. In his diary on his first visit he wrote 'Nothing in Abergavenny worth seeing', an opinion he later revised when in 1798 he painted *Abergavenny Bridge: Clearing Up after a Showery Day.*

Many other people of local and national renown are more closely connected with the county.

Adam of Usk (about 1360-1430)
Most of the information about Adam comes from his own *Chronicon Adae de Usk,* which recounts his life. He was a student at Oxford and became a lecturer and lawyer. He rose to prominence in the church and served under Pope Boniface IX. His chronicles are interesting in that they also record contemporary events such as the Battle of Agincourt in 1415. He is commemorated in Usk church.

Aneurin Bevan (1897-1960)
'Nye' Bevan was born in Tredegar, the son of a miner, and became a collier's helper at thirteen. In 1929 he was elected Labour member of Parliament for Ebbw Vale. As Minister of Health in the 1945 Labour government he was the architect of the National Health Service. He was also involved in the implementation of the National Insurance scheme and leader of the left-wing group of the Labour Party. He was well known for his impassioned oratory and was sometimes so rude to opponents that Churchill called him a 'merchant of discourtesy'.

On the hillside outside Tredegar stand the Aneurin Bevan Memorial Stones. On the central stone is inscribed: 'From this spot Aneurin Bevan spoke to the people of his constituency and the world'. The others face the towns which he represented and are inscribed 'Tredegar', 'Ebbw Vale' and 'Rhymney'. In Bedwelty House in the town can be seen a finely sculptured bust of Bevan.

W. H. Davies (1871-1940)

William Henry Davies, the 'tramp poet', was born in a pub in Newport on 20th April 1871. Abandoning an apprenticeship in the picture-frame business, he went to America, where he lived as a tramp for six years doing casual work and travelling about by 'jumping' trains. A train unfortunately severed one of his legs, but he continued to travel in cattle boats before returning to Britain where he lived in penury. After eight years he published and sold his first book of poems. His *Autobiography of a Super Tramp* brought him to public notice. His output of poems and prose continued until his death. If for nothing else, he will always be remembered for the couplet in his short poem *Leisure:*

'A poor life this if, full of care,
We have no time to stand and stare.'

John Frost (1784-1877)

John Frost was a tailor and draper in Newport. He became a councillor and magistrate in 1835 and mayor of Newport the following year. He campaigned for a people's charter and was prominent in the movement which became known as Chartism. Disquiet was growing in Gwent (and throughout Britain) and in May 1839 a detachment of soldiers was sent to Newport. On 3rd November the Chartists began to gather for a mass demonstration. The authorities arrested many known Chartists in Newport and swore in 500 special constables. Frost gathered a body of men from the valley towns and marched towards Newport. The demonstration reached Newport on the morning of 4th November and went to the Westgate Inn to demand the release of the arrested men. There is conflicting evidence about what happened next, but fighting began and shots rang out. The soldiers fired into the crowd, which fled. 22 people were killed.

John Frost, Zephaniah Williams of Nantyglo and William Jones of Pontypool were arrested and later tried and found guilty of high treason at Monmouth. They were sentenced to death by drawing, hanging, having their heads cut off and bodies quartered. Three weeks later, after the gallows had been constructed, the sentences were commuted to transportation for life. They were sent to Van Dieman's Land (Tasmania). In 1854 they received conditional pardons and Frost returned to Newport in 1856 amid great celebration, at the age of 72. He was given a magnificent reception in London.

Geoffrey of Monmouth (?1100-54)

Geoffrey probably received his education in the Benedictine priory of Monmouth. He became an archdeacon in the diocese of Llandaff and Bishop of St Asaph. However, he is known to posterity as the author of the remarkable romantic volume *Historia Britonum,* a legendary history of British kings, completed about 1147 and compiled from the writings of Nennius and from a Celtic book of Breton legends. For a long time it was considered real history but later it was shown to be largely fabulous; however, it has been widely plundered by later writers, poets and romancers seeking material for their own work. A window (known locally as Geoffrey's Window) in the youth hostel at Monmouth is said to look out from his library; however, it dates from several centuries after his death.

Sir Benjamin Hall (1802-67)

Benjamin Hall was married to Augusta Waddington of Llanover House. He was created Lord Llanover in 1859 and played an active part in government. Among the many ministerial appointments he held was that of Chief Commissioner of Works in Lord Aberdeen's government and his nickname, 'Big Ben', was adopted for the bell of the Houses of Parliament. It is for this that he is chiefly remembered.

Part of the mural of the Chartist Uprising, 1839, John Frost Square, Newport.

37

Henry V (1388-1422)

The only king of England to have been born in Gwent, Henry was born at Monmouth Castle on 9th August 1387. His father was then the Earl of Derby and there seemed little possibility of either succeeding to the throne. When his father seized the throne from Richard II, Harry of Monmouth was created Prince of Wales and he succeeded to the crown in 1413.

Rudolf Hess (born 1894)

Rudolf Hess was second in command to Hitler in Nazi Germany. In May 1941 he flew to Scotland, where his plane crashed and he was taken prisoner by the British authorities. For the duration of the war he was held in Britain, much of the time at Maindiff Court in Abergavenny. He was allowed out under armed guard and one of his favourite places to visit was White Castle. On one of these outings he signed a beer mat for the proprietor of a local pub. This is now in Abergavenny Museum. Hess is serving a life sentence for war crimes in Spandau Prison, Berlin.

Father Ignatius (1837-1908)

Father Ignatius was born Joseph Leycester Lyne, who dreamed of becoming 'no ordinary clergyman'. He was convinced that everything he did was directly inspired by God, which alienated him from his superiors in the Church of England. Lyne wished to revive monasticism within the Church of England, based on the monastic order of St Benedict. He was attracted to the Vale of Ewyas, where he had seen the ruins of Llanthony Priory, but the owners refused to sell. Ignatius chose a site higher up the valley at Capel-y-ffin to establish his monastery. He was extremely eloquent and raised money by making preaching tours. In 1880 apparitions were seen and in 1936 a calvary was set up to mark the spot. A pilgrimage takes place annually 'to the glory of God, in honour of Our Lady and in memory of Father Ignatius as a holy man' (see chapter 9).

Walter Savage Landor (1775-1864)

Walter Savage Landor was a poet who was so taken with the Vale of Ewyas that he purchased Llanthony Abbey and the estates surrounding it in 1802. He built himself a house looking down on the abbey (little of it remains today) and planted many of the fine trees which can still be seen. Landor's ferocious temper antagonised his neighbours and tenants so he sold the estate in 1814 and spent much of the rest of his life abroad. He wrote of the estate:

'Llanthony! An ungenial clime...
I loved thee by thy streams of yore,
By distant streams I love thee more...'

Saint David Lewis (1617-79)

David Lewis was the son of the headmaster of the grammar school in Abergavenny and became a Catholic and then a Jesuit. He carried on his religious work in South Wales in the face of growing persecution. He ministered to the Gunter family, who lived in Abergavenny, and other families in the county. Following the Titus Oates plot, he was arrested at Llantarnam in November 1678. After much prevarication he was put to death at Usk for practising his faith and is said to be buried just outside Usk church. He was canonised in 1929. There is a memorial stained glass window to him and other local martyrs in the Roman Catholic church in Abergavenny.

Statues of Charles Rolls and Henry the Fifth in Agincourt Square, Monmouth.

HENRY V.
BORN MONMOUTH
AUG 9 1387

Lady Llanover (1803-96)
Augusta Waddington was married to Sir Benjamin Hall, Lord Llanover ('Big Ben'), but was a remarkable lady in her own right. She was an ardent supporter of all things Welsh. Welsh was spoken in her household and the tenants of the estate were native speakers. Her servants were dressed in traditional Welsh costume and a mill was established in Llanover to weave indigenous patterned flannel. She also had a resident harpist to play the triple-stringed harp, an instrument peculiar to Wales.

Lady Llanover was a founder member of the Cymreigyddion y Fenni in 1833 (the word Cymreigyddion means 'a society of Welshmen'). This society became a movement to revitalise Welsh culture and established the annual Eisteddfod programmes which continue to this day. She gave encouragement by offering prize money of £5 for the best collections of Welsh flannels 'in real National checks and stripes with the Welsh names by which they are known...' Lady Llanover was given the bardic title 'Gwenynen Gwent' (the 'Bee of Gwent'). She also published a number of books and was involved in the formation of the Welsh Manuscript Society.

Henry Marten (1602-80)
Henry Marten was known as 'the Regicide' from his having been one of the signatories to the death warrant of Charles I. It is said that after having signed the warrant Cromwell splashed Marten's face with ink in passing the pen and that Marten retaliated by bespattering Cromwell. At the Restoration of the monarchy Marten was tried and sentenced to twenty years imprisonment. He was kept in captivity in Chepstow Castle in Bigod's Tower, which henceforth became known as Marten's Tower. He died in prison and was buried in St Mary's Church, Chepstow.

Charles Stewart Rolls (1877-1910)
Rolls was the son of Lord and Lady Llangattock of The Hendre near Monmouth. He showed a practical interest in mechanical things from an early age and supervised the wiring of The Hendre for electricity. He studied mechanics and applied science at Cambridge. In 1894, while on holiday in Paris, he saw his first car and bought one two years later. He drove home from Cambridge for Christmas, taking three days for the journey. It was the first time a car had been seen in Monmouth. He became interested in racing and came second in the Paris to Ostend race in 1899. In 1902 he set up a car sales and repair firm, C. S. Rolls and Company in Fulham and two years later started to sell the 10 horsepower car made by Henry Royce. It was the first car to bear the name 'Rolls-Royce'. The two firms amalgamated in 1906 and the first Rolls-Royce Silver Ghost appeared at the Motor Show that year.

Motoring was becoming such a reliable mode of travel that Rolls sought a new challenge. He found it in ballooning and then in flying. He was the first British airman to fly more than half a mile (800 metres) and he was the first man to make a double crossing of the English Channel, in June 1910. While taking part in an air display in Bournemouth on 12th July 1910 his plane plummeted to the ground and he was killed, the first British aviator to die in a plane crash. A statue commemorating his achievement stands in Agincourt Square, Monmouth; it was unveiled on 19th October 1911.

Edward Somerset (1601-67)
Edward Somerset was the son of the first Marquis of Worcester but, unusually for an aristocrat, he is remembered not for his part in politics but as the author of a book called *A Century of Inventions* (1633). The 68th invention was the principle of the steam engine. The book was described as 'a list of a hundred projects most of them impossibilities'. He was buried in Raglan church (see chapter 10).

Sidney Gilchrist Thomas (1850-85)
Thomas was born in London, the son of a Welsh civil servant. He left school at seventeen because of his father's death but continued to study chemistry in evening classes, where it was mentioned that the man who could eliminate phosphorus in the Bessemer convertor would make his fortune. This fired Thomas's imagination. By 1877 he believed he had found the answer and spent his weekends in Blaenavon Ironworks experimenting with his cousin Percy Gilchrist, the works chemist. In association with E. P. Martin, the manager, they proved Thomas's technique worked. Great interest was taken and Andrew Carnegie bought the patents to the process for a quarter of a million dollars. A memorial at the works in Forgeside commemorates Thomas's discoveries.

Dr Alfred Russel Wallace (1823-1913)
Wallace was a native of Usk and became an eminent naturalist. His *Travels on the Amazon* was published in 1853. His theory of evolution was thought out during an illness on an insect-collecting expedition in the Moluccas and his first ideas on the subject were sent to Darwin in England. A joint paper was read to the Linnean Society but it is Darwin's ideas, published in *The Origin of Species*, which are better known today.

9
Folklore, customs and events

The folklore of Gwent has many similarities with stories related in the neighbouring counties of Herefordshire and Glamorgan, and some of these themes will be found throughout Wales and Britain. Many of the legends evolved to explain natural phenomena or remains left by early man that people could not comprehend.

Other folk tales seem to have grown up to discourage children from doing dangerous things, like playing near water. One wonders if a story recounted by William Coxe during his tour of Monmouthshire in 1801 regarding the Newcastle oak grew up to prevent people from damaging a magnificent tree. It used to stand near the pub in the village and was said to be protected by fairies. Anyone who dared to cut wood from it would become a victim of the fairies' revenge. One person fell from the tree and broke his arm in trying to chop down a branch, another fractured a leg, while a third 'perished shortly after his sacriligious enterprise by an untimely death'.

There are many different tales told about the Skirrid (Ysgyrydd Fawr) or Holy Mountain near Abergavenny. It is a steep-sided ridge with two landslips on it. The legends attempt to provide an explanation for these features. One version is that they were caused by the earthquake which happened at the time of Christ's crucifixion, another that as Noah was sailing over in the Ark the tip of the mountain was knocked off by the boat.

Another natural feature which has a tale about it is the limestone pillar (OS 162, SO 543995) which stands out from the cliffs high above the Wye. It is not actually in Gwent but it was from here that the devil was supposed to have preached to the monks at Tintern Abbey below to tempt them away from their toils devoted to God. The outcrop is known as the 'Devil's Pulpit'. One day the devil became even bolder and dared to descend and enter the abbey. The monks threw holy water on him, which scalded him, and he fled in pain, not stopping until he had leapt the river at Llandogo, leaving the marks of his talons on a stone.

The Dial Garreg or Stone of Revenge near Cwmyoy (OS 161, SO 285241) recalls a historical event which is recorded by Giraldus Cambrensis. The stone stands near a wood called Coed Dinas, which may have been the Coed Grone which Giraldus mentions. Shortly after the death of Henry I, Richard de Clare was travelling through Wales accompanied by Brian de Wallingford, Lord of Abergavenny, and an armed guard. Near the wood de Clare dismissed Wallingford and the men-at-arms and proceeded on his journey with only a minstrel and a singer. An ambush by the Welsh awaited them and the whole party was slaughtered.

A landmark near Clydach (OS 161, SO 219144) is known as the Lonely Shepherd. It is a limestone pillar left after quarrying in the vicinity. The legend woven around it tells of a shepherd who was so cruel to his wife that she drowned herself in the river Usk. The shepherd was turned to stone for his evil character, except for a few hours on Midsummer Night when he goes down to the river to search for his wife. Before dawn he is restored to his solitary position on the skyline.

Jack of Kent is a character who appears in many stories relating to Gwent (and other counties) and may be based on Sion Cent, a Welsh poet who flourished in the fifteenth century. He was always in some tussle with the devil, whom he usually managed to outwit. Together they were said to be responsible for building Grosmont bridge. Jack got the devil to carry stones for the bridge, which was being built during the night. One night the devil was caught unawares by the dawn whilst still carrying stones. At the moment the cock crowed he dropped the stones he was carrying and they can still be seen on the common between Garway and Grosmont.

Another incident between the two occurred when the devil challenged Jack to a stone-throwing contest from Trelleck Beacon. Jack had the first throw, then the devil heaved his a little further but Jack managed a third, more distant throw. Where they landed the Trelleck stones stand today.

CUSTOMS

There were many customs in the county which have disappeared over the years. When couples were getting married many people were invited to the wedding and the guests would provide money gifts to set the newlyweds up in their new life together. At Nantyglo, Blaina, Tredegar, Rhymney and other valley towns, it is recorded that after the marriage banns had been read friends would be invited to a *pastau* at a local pub where cooked pies and ale would be consumed. A small sum of money would be charged and the *pastau* would continue for a number of days. The money collected would allow the couple to set up home for themselves.

In Tredegar unfaithful husbands and wives were tied to a plank and carried through the streets. One such procession was stopped by the local police in Chepstow in January 1865.

40

LEFT: *Harold's Stones, Trelleck.*

ABOVE: *A painting of the Mari Lwyd on the signboard of Llanover Post Office.*

The rituals surrounding the Mari Lwyd, essentially a Welsh custom, have died out since the nineteenth century but a reminder of these New Year activities is a painting of the Mari Lwyd displayed on the exterior of Llanover post office. The Mari Lwyd was a horse's skull or a carved block of wood mounted on a pole and decorated with white sheeting, ribbons and bells. It was carried round from house to house by a small party of young men who sang outside each home whilst those inside attempted to out-sing them. Eventually the door would be opened and the Mari Lwyd allowed in to entertain the assembled company, and the party would be welcomed with cakes and beer. It was a custom widespread throughout Gwent but seems to have died out with the decline of Welsh speaking in the area.

The Calennig was another New Year custom which continued well into the twentieth century. The Calennig was an apple pierced with four sticks, three to form legs and the fourth to provide a handle. It was studded with golden grains of corn and decorated with a sprig of holly, on which were hung split hazelnuts. This was then carried around the village by children singing carols, who visited each household,

where they received small gifts of money or food, after which they called out 'Blwyddyn Newydd Dda' (Happy New Year). Around the Chepstow area the Calennig was known as the 'Monty'.

St David's Day (1st March) is celebrated throughout Wales by people wearing either a leek or, more usually, a daffodil in their buttonholes. Younger children go to school wearing what is believed to be the traditional Welsh costume — checked Welsh flannel skirts with an apron and a flannel shawl, and a tall black hat trimmed with lace. At Llanover school the day is also celebrated by dancing the 'Llanover Reel', a traditional dance kept alive by Lady Llanover, who encouraged Welsh customs.

EVENTS
March
The Three Peaks Trial: an 18 mile (29 km) walk starting and finishing at Bailey Park car park, Abergavenny, taking in the three mountain peaks around the town — the Blorenge, Sugar Loaf and Skirrid. Last Saturday in March.

41

The 'Llanover Reel' performed by the Pontypool Folk Dance group outside Caldicot castle.

May

Llantilio Crossenny Festival of Music: held in the parish church, where recitals are given by professional musicians. First weekend in May and the preceding weekdays.

Steam Rally with veteran and vintage cars, Baily Park, Abergavenny. Spring Bank Holiday weekend, Saturday and Sunday.

British Horse Society Horse Trials: two-day event at Piercefield Park, Chepstow Racecourse.

July

The Welsh Derby, Chepstow Racecourse. Second Tuesday in July

Abergavenny and Border Counties Show, Llanwenarth Citra, near Abergavenny. Last Saturday in July.

August

Chepstow Agricultural Show, Chepstow Racecourse. First Saturday in August.

The Kymin Dash: a class 'C' fell race, starting from Monmouth Leisure Centre, racing through the town to the top of the Kymin and finishing on Chippenham meadows. A Satur-

day in mid August.

Father Ignatius Pilgrimage: Holy Eucharist at St David's church, Llanthony, at 11.30 a.m.; procession from Capel-y-ffin church to the abbey church at the monastery, at 2.30 p.m. A Saturday in late August.

Royal Monmouthshire Agricultural Show, Monmouth. Last Saturday in August.

September

Wye River Raft Race: held over a 6 mile (10 km) course starting at Monmouth Boathouse and finishing at Whitebrook. First Saturday in September.

Usk Agricultural Show. Second Saturday of September.

Pandy Ploughing Match: changing venue each year. For information telephone the secretary Gill Lewis: telephone Cross Ash (087 386) 224. The event includes ploughing by horses and vintage tractors and sheep dog trials. Second Saturday in September.

December

The Welsh National, Chepstow Racecourse. The Saturday before Christmas.

42

10
Towns and villages

ABERGAVENNY

Abergavenny grew up on a low hill left by the retreating glaciers in the valley of the Usk, where the river Gavenny flows into the Usk (hence the name of the town). Finds of Roman remains indicate that Abergavenny was the Roman fort of *Gobannium* named in Antonine's Itinerary. Archaeological excavations during the 1960s confirmed this and located the site of the fort to the west of the ruins of the Norman castle.

The castle was established in about 1090 by Hamelin de Ballon, who also founded a priory. A town (inhabited by Anglo-Saxon and Norman settlers) rapidly grew up to serve as a market for the castle, priory and surrounding area. To protect the town against the native Welsh it was defended by a wall with four gates. None of these gates survives today; the last one was pulled down in the nineteenth century to widen the road. Today their positions are recorded by wall plaques.

Within the walls stood the parish church of St John, which at the Dissolution was endowed to become the King Henry VIII Grammar School. Although religious services continued to be held there in Welsh, the congregation used the priory church of St Mary as the parish church. St John's was used as a school until 1898, when a new school building was completed. It then became a masonic temple and remains so to this day.

The present size of Abergavenny belies its former importance. In the past its wealth was based on the agriculture of the surrounding district and its role as market town and commercial centre. Other important industries included the leather trade with its allied crafts of tanning and boot and shoe manufacturing, glove making and flannel weaving. In the late eighteenth and nineteenth centuries it benefited from the increasing industrialisation in the neighbouring mountains and in the mid nineteenth century became a flourishing railway town.

Much of the town appears to date from the late eighteenth or early nineteenth century but frequently the facades hide much older buildings and its streets are well worth exploring. Two of particular note are Nevill Street and Market Street. Nevill Street, formerly called Rother Street (named after the Welsh black cattle which were sold in the street), is predominantly of eighteenth-century appearance (one notable building is a shop (number 16) which was formerly a pub called the Cow Inn. It was built in the fifteenth or sixteenth century as a sizable merchant's house belonging to the Vaughan family, whose arms are displayed in the intricately carved window sills. In the late eighteenth century a third storey was added and this was when it became the Cow Inn and acquired carved cows' heads just below the eaves. Market Street is a small terrace of medieval timber-framed and jettied buildings approached by a raised pavement.

The town is dominated by the clock tower of the town hall and market place which was completed in 1870 in the Gothic style. Abergavenny's enduring importance lies in the continuance of a thriving market. General markets are held on Tuesdays and Fridays when the streets are thronged with shoppers from near and far.

BLACKWOOD

Although there is little evidence of it today, Blackwood started as a planned village. It was the idea of John Hodder Moggridge, who lived at Llanrumney Hall until he built a new mansion called Woodfield in the Sirhowy valley. He was a social philanthropist who sought to improve the lot of the poor by providing them with the means to help themselves. His 'village system' plan was evolved in consultation with a number of persons including Robert Owen. The idea was to select industrious farm labourers and colliers 'who had been able with difficulty to maintain themselves and their families when in health and full work' and to offer each a lease on a piece of ground. The conditions were that a small ground rent was paid, a substantial cottage built, a garden laid out, and loans advanced by Moggridge repaid with interest. The landlord would clear the site and building stone would be available from quarries on his estate.

The idea was slow to catch on and only three men initially accepted leases. In the spring of 1820 gardens were planted with potatoes and by midsummer three cottages were occupied. It took two years before other people realised the advantages of the scheme and particularly the great value of a productive garden. All the tenants were able to repay the debts. By June 1822 a further thirty houses had been built. Moggridge then erected a market house for the village which was opened in October 1822. It had a meeting place, later used as a nonconformist chapel and school room. Each year apart from 1827 more houses were added; shops and an inn were opened and various tradesmen settled there.

The wood originally cleared for the village was Y Coed Duon, the 'Black Wood' from

43

which the town derived its name. In an advertisement in *The Cambrian* in 1822 the place was called 'the new village in the Blackwood' and in the paper's report of the inauguration of the market house it was referred to as 'the village of Tre-Moggridge' but by 1829 it was known by its present name.

Another, smaller village was established on similar lines at **Ynys-ddu,** a few miles down the Sirhowy valley, and after a road was constructed down the Rhymney valley from the ironworks another village called Tre-lyn was also laid out. Today this village is called **Fleur-de-lis.**

BLAENAVON

Blaenavon grew up at the head of the Afon Lwyd valley, hence its name (*Blaen,* head of; *avon* or *afon,* river). The town is over 1000 feet (300 metres) above sea level with the open moorland of the mountains surrounding it — the Blorenge, Coity Mountain and Mynydd-y-Garn-fawr.

Until the 1780s the area was inhabited by a few scattered hill farmers; then three Midland entrepreneurs, Thomas Hill, Thomas Hopkins and Benjamin Pratt, leased the land knowing that all the raw materials (iron ore, coal and limestone) for ironmaking were to be found in the vicinity. An ironworks was established and by the end of the eighteenth century the population had grown to more than 2000.

Production at the ironworks reached its peak in the 1820s. By 1900 the original ironworks (see chapter 7) was replaced by another plant on the other side of the valley. The town was also served by several coal mines in the area, the closest being Big Pit, which was closed in 1980 and reopened as a mining museum (see chapter 6).

Broad Street, the main commercial area and the surrounding terraces are typical of a South Wales industrial valley town. Various buildings in the town stand as a reminder of its industrial past. Ty Mawr, 'Big House', was built as the residence of Samuel Hopkins, one of the early proprietors of the ironworks, during the first decade of the nineteenth century. It was used by the Blaenavon Company until 1924 and then became the town's hospital. St Peter's School was built and endowed by Sarah Hopkins, as a memorial to her brother, Samuel, who had died the previous year. It opened in 1816 with 120 pupils and was the first purpose-built school paid for by an industrial family in Wales.

The Workmen's Hall and Institute is a fine example of a community hall. It was completed in 1894 and was entirely financed by voluntary contributions from private individuals and the Blaenavon Company. Other buildings of interest are St Peter's church (see chapter 5) and the Horeb Chapel, which was built in 1862.

St Peter's School, Blaenavon.

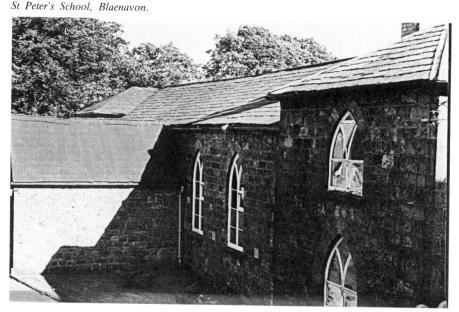

44

Black Rank Cottages, Blaenavon.

The Blaenavon Ironworks established on the other side of the valley is where Sidney Gilchrist Thomas (see chapter 8) first succeeded in using phosphoric ores in the Bessemer steelmaking process. To house the workers, a small village called Forgeside was built around a village green, and the streets were unimaginatively termed A, B, C, D and E rows. A and B were demolished in 1977 but the others still survive.

BLAINA and NANTYGLO

The villages of Blaina and Nantyglo grew during the industrial revolution and for many years were important centres of ironmaking and coal mining. Today they form an almost continuous built-up area running south from Brynmawr within a steeply sided valley. The Nantyglo Ironworks was established by Richard Harford and Company in 1795 but investment problems forced closure within a year. The main growth began in 1811 when Joseph and Crawshay Bailey acquired the works and operated it in conjunction with the Beaufort works which they also owned.

Joseph Bailey built a house at Nantyglo near the site of a more modest dwelling previously constructed by Harford. It had marvellous views southwards down the valley. The house no longer exists but the foundations have been excavated. No evidence of a tunnel said to connect the house to one of two fortified towers (built about 1820) has yet been found. The remnants of these two towers, built in the vicinity of the house near to farm buildings (where the Baileys were said to have housed blackleg labour), can still be seen. The towers were probably built to intimidate the local workforce rather than to protect the family in

case of violence breaking out. They can be seen on the western banks of the Ebbw Fach river, just south of the comprehensive school. The more complete of the two has been renovated and it is hoped to establish an interpretative trail around the area.

On the opposite side of the valley stood a line of terraced houses called Bayliss Row. Crawshay Bailey was known as an autocratic, tight-fisted employer, a reputation borne out by the existence of these houses. They were minute two-roomed houses, smaller than any others built in Gwent around the same date (about 1827). All the windows and doors were inserted on the uphill side of the row so that the inhabitants could not overlook the ironmaster's mansion.

There was much unrest leading up to the Chartist riots of 1839. One of the leaders of the march to Newport was Zephaniah Williams, who kept the Royal Oak pub at Blaina.

At Blaina, the ironworks was established in 1823 and three furnaces were producing 2400 tons in 1825. It later became part of the Nantyglo and Blaina Iron Company. Many collieries were opened in Blaina and in 1827 the Henwaen Pit was the scene of a disastrous explosion which killed 21 men and boys.

Blaina and Nantyglo grew to provide housing for the workmen of the ironworks and the pits. For the proprietors this was an era of great prosperity and Thomas Hill of the Blaenavon Ironworks said that 'the Nant-y-glo people are coining money, aye, rolling banknotes'.

BRYNMAWR

The name of the town means 'Big Hill' and Brynmawr is situated at the head of both the

45

Bailey's tower, Nantyglo.

Health established in England and Wales in 1851. Although many industrial towns were squalid during their growth years it was particularly noted in 1853 that the interiors of houses in Brynmawr were very clean: 'the rooms are swept, the floors whited, and the furniture and kitchen utensils bright and clean'.

A similar spirit of enterprise existed during the depression years of the 1920s and 1930s. An attempt at reconstruction was made, called the 'Brynmawr Experiment'. In 1928, when the resources of the Town Distress Committee were nearly exhausted, help was given by the Quakers to try to diminish reliance on coal mining. A Community Study Council was formed with the aim 'to create that ideal community in which every individual can have the best and fullest life and to which all contribute'. The first step was the formation of a small boot-making group financed by a loan from the Co-operative Society.

In 1930 the Brynmawr and Clydach Valley Industries Limited was registered to enquire into the possibility of starting new industries, to raise capital and to gather together businessmen of proved ability to provide expertise. A furniture-making group was also formed. This enterprise was made possible by bringing in skilled craftsmen and designers. Brynmawr furniture can still be seen in homes today and several pieces are in the National Museum of Wales. This whole scheme came to an end during the Second World War.

industrial valley of the Ebbw Fach which runs southwards and the Clydach valley which runs eastwards. Originally it lay in Breconshire and then was incorporated into Monmouthshire, which subsequently became Gwent. To the north of the town is the open moorland of the Brecon Beacons. The old Welsh name for the place was *Waun Helygen* (marsh of the willow). Like many towns of the area, until as late as 1800 it was a small hamlet which expanded with the growth of local industry.

Many workers at Clydach, Nantyglo and Beaufort ironworks made their homes at Brynmawr, which stood at the intersection of roads and tramroads which carried the raw materials and products of industries. The coach road from Abergavenny to Merthyr, which was the shortest route from England to the South Wales coalfield, ran through Brynmawr.

The intersecting tramroads provided a skeleton town plan. Houses grew up along the tracks and as the town is situated on a spacious plateau it was able to develop on all sides. Since it grew as a dormitory town for those who worked elsewhere, the houses were built by individuals and tradesmen. It was a progressive town in that it had the first Board of

CAERLEON

Caerleon is a small town on the banks of the Usk about 3 miles (5 km) north-east of Newport. During Roman times it was an important legionary fortress known as *Isca*, a latinised form of the name of the Usk. The present name records the town's past, *caer* meaning 'fortress' and *leon* 'of the legion'. It was the station of the Second Augustan Legion, which came from Strasbourg to take part in the invasion of Britain in AD 43. The building of the fortress started in AD 75 with an earth bank protecting an area of about 50 acres (20 ha) with the headquarters, stores and barracks inside and a civil settlement with houses, shops, workshops, temples, cemeteries and an amphitheatre outside. As Caerleon has remained relatively small in subsequent centuries there is still much evidence of the Roman occupation (see chapter 3). Giraldus Cambrensis visited the town towards the end of the twelfth century and commented that 'You may still see here many vestiges of former splendour; immense palaces with golden pediments...a gigantic tower; extraordinary hot baths; remains of temples and places for theatrical performances...subterranean buildings, aqueducts and underground passages.'

Before the Norman invasion Caerleon was the principal town of a Welsh kingdom and the seat of Caradoc ap Gruffydd. When Caradoc died about 1070 he was succeeded by his son Owan Wan (the weak), who is supposed to have surrendered his power to the Normans. The Normans built a motte and bailey in the south-east corner of the Roman fortress walls, known as the Mynde. Traditionally it has been regarded as the site of King Arthur's palace and Arthur's Tower stood on top of this mound. The mound is now in the garden of a private residence but fragments of a bailey wall can be traced behind the present Baptist chapel to a ruined round tower which once guarded the medieval bridge or river crossing.

The town received a charter from the de Clares and it was renewed at frequent intervals between 1324 and 1497. The importance of Caerleon depended on its position as a distribution centre and its close links with Bristol. In the eighteenth century a plate works was established at Caerleon and products were shipped from the quay near the bridge.

The Hanbury Arms, which stands near the bridge, was originally the town house of the Morgan family before they moved to Llantarnam Abbey about 1593. Remains of the round tower can still be seen incorporated into the building. It once had a companion on the opposite side of the river. Before the present stone bridge of three arches (which was built in 1866 despite the tablet bearing the date 1800, which came from a bridge in Newport constructed by the same builder, David Edwards) the river was crossed by a wooden bridge. In 1772 it was washed away in a flood and an old woman named Williams was carried as far as Newport on the timbers before her lantern attracted attention and rescue. Across the bridge is Caerleon-ultra-Pontem, known as 'the village'.

At the junction of Cross Street and High Street stands the Bull Inn, of sixteenth-century origin but much altered. Near here once stood the market hall and cross but the market was demolished in 1848. Opposite the Bull Inn stands the priory though there is no evidence to connect it with the old abbey at Llantarnam. Opposite the parish church is Caerleon Endowed School, established in 1724 by the Williams Charity. Today Caerleon is mainly a residential town with the large hospital of St Cadoc's and a teacher training college started in 1912.

CAERWENT

The name of this village means 'camp of the west'. Today it is a quiet village gathered

The Roman Amphitheatre, Caerleon.

around a church and set in a gently rolling countryside. However, in Roman times it was *Venta Silurnum*, the civil township or market town which was established by the Romans when they were building *Isca* at Caerleon. It was the only such town established in Wales. It became a stipendiary and paid a tribute to the Romans. Its earliest mention is in Antonine's Itinerary.

The Roman settlement had a rectangular layout covering 44 acres (18 ha) divided by a main road running east to west with two smaller roads running in the same direction and four running north to south, dividing the town into twenty blocks of *insulae*. It contained a forum or market place, a *basilica* (town hall), bath buildings, a temple, shops and houses. The road running straight through the village runs straight through the Roman town. The northern gateway to the town has been cleared and can be seen beside the village inn. There were originally four gates. The wall is traceable all the way round and in parts is still easily seen (see chapter 3).

In 1912 a stone coffin was discovered containing a human skeleton. This was thought to be the remains of St Tathan, who is reputed to have founded a school or monastery at Caerwent in the sixth century. The coffin and remains were moved to the south aisle of the parish church and a slab was laid over them inscribed in Latin to commemorate the holy man. Since this date numerous other skeletons have been found, showing the place to have been the site of the Roman cemetery outside the walls of the town.

In Norman times a motte was constructed in the east corner of the southern wall, but no more building seems to have taken place. In the sixteenth century Leland wrote: 'It was some time a faire and large cyte. The places where the iiii gates was yet standith but all to minischyde and torne. Within and aboute the waulle be a xvi or xvii small houses for husbandmen, of new making'.

The church dedicated to St Stephen dates from the thirteenth century and the stonework appears to consist largely of material from former Roman buildings. It contains a magnificently carved oak pulpit inscribed with the words 'Woe be to me if I priach not the gospel 1632'.

Near the Roman east gate is a block of almshouses built in 1912 for old and infirm women.

CHEPSTOW

Chepstow was known in Norman times as *Striguil*. It is situated at the south-east corner of the county at a crossing point on the river Wye, about 3 miles (5 km) north of where the Wye flows into the Severn estuary. The positions of both the town and the castle are remarkable. The castle has a dramatic location on the cliffs overlooking the river. It was established by William Fitz Osbern before 1071 (see chapter 4).

Seen from the Gloucester road as it drops down to the river bridge, the castle ruins dominate the scene and it is difficult to distinguish where the limestone cliff ends and the masonry begins. The builders of the castle skilfully used the natural terrain to make it a seemingly impregnable fortress. On the south side the land drops away and is separated from the town by a ravine, probably deepened by the extraction of stone for building the castle walls. This valley is now laid out as a pleasant public park called the Dell.

The town is built on the steep hill rising away from the river. It grew up as a market centre as its name indicates, being derived from the Old English *ceap stow*, meaning market place. The settlement was protected by a defensive wall called the Portwall which originally ran around the town from the castle to the river bank with only one entrance. This was the Town Gate, which was built in the late thirteenth century and still stands today although in an altered state (it was called 'New Gate' in 1573). It served as a toll gate as well as a fortified entrance to the town. In 1687 the tolls were: "All Shoemakers, Smyths, Iron mongers, Hatters, Glovers and Pedlars are respectively on the Faire dayh to pay....1 penny. For every peece of linnen cloth or fflannel brought under peoples Armes to be sold 1 penny...For all sorts of Grayne sold in the market of Chepstow aforesaid out of every sack conteyning four bushells or more a quarter Peck Winchester measure...'

Paddy Magill, the last toll collector, died in 1874. The annual fairs and weekly markets used to be held in Beaufort Square, which is in the middle of the town.

As well as the market Chepstow traded as a port. From medieval times it had close trading links with Bristol. There was a great trade in timber from the Wye valley and oak bark was stored in the riverside warehouses for shipping to Irish tanneries. Shipbuilding and ropemaking were also important industries which declined during the nineteenth century but briefly revived during the First World War. As a result of the wartime expansion in the shipyards 20,000 workers were brought into Chepstow and three 'garden cities' were built to house them at Hardwick, Bulwark and Pennsylvania.

Chepstow has a number of interesting buildings, not least being the elegant iron road bridge built in 1816 by John Rennie to span the Wye. The buildings fronting the river bank are warehouses for earlier river traffic. Just downstream from the road bridge is the railway bridge, a tubular suspension bridge

Chepstow, looking towards the town gate.

designed by Isambard Kingdom Brunel (who also designed the station) and opened in 1852. Further up the hill into the town are St Mary's church (see chapter 5) and two almshouses. The one in Upper Church Street was founded by Sir Walter Montagu in 1614 and the other in Bridge Street was founded by Thomas Powis in 1716.

The Wye is famous for its salmon which have been fished for centuries. At Chepstow they are caught in bag-shaped stop nets which are hung from two poles from a moored boat.

CWMBRAN

Cwmbran is the first new town in Wales, built at the southern end of the Afon Llwyd valley. During the 1930s the decline of traditional industries led to great poverty. Central government made efforts to remedy the situation by encouraging new industries to come to the valley. These new industries and almost full employment led to the need for more housing. The new town absorbed existing small villages such as Cwmbran and Llantarnam and created a new landscape of modern architecture in what had been an agricultural area. The new town consists of seven residential neighbourhoods and a town centre. Each neighbourhood has its own local shopping centre and schools so that children do not have to walk far. All the roads within the neighbourhoods were designed with the safety of residents of paramount importance and speed of vehicle movement secondary.

The town centre is encircled by a one-way road system with ample multi-storey car parks on the outskirts. These are connected to the shopping areas by pedestrian ways and underpasses which completely segregate vehicles and pedestrians. The town centre is set out in a rectilinear grid pattern of shopping malls and squares with the Congress Theatre and a bandstand in one square. The only part not conforming to this grid is the old house of Llantarnam Grange, which is now a gallery and social centre.

Gwent House, a block of residential flats, is decorated with sculptures in relief panels by Henry Collins illustrating the history of Gwent. Another interesting building is an old hostelry called the Green House at Llantarnam, sited on the main road from Newport to Pontypool. The doorway is flanked by two large flamboyant barley-sugar twist columns and over the door is a wood carving of two men sitting at a table drinking. An inscription reads: 'The Green House 1719 / good Beer / And Cider for you / Come in / You shall taste it.'

49

EBBW VALE

Ebbw Vale is situated at the head of the valley of the Ebbw Fawr river. In 1778 the entire population of the valley was about 140 people but in that year the Duke of Beaufort leased land to Kendall and Company to build an iron furnace, which changed the whole valley. The works were called the Beaufort Ironworks in honour of the ground landlord. In 1919 it was described as 'the strangest landscapes in these islands . . . There are two mountains facing one another and on the skirts of the nearest hangs the town which is named after the valley, with its ironworks below. Across the hollow are terraces of white cottages ruled on the hillside as with a ruler, and the brown mountain stretches behind them . . . the black heaps have thrown up fantastic curves and peaks . . .'

Ebbw Vale Ironworks was established in 1790 and it later became a steelworks. In its heyday the plant covered a distance of 3 miles (5 km), comprising Bessemer and open hearth works, blast furnaces, coke ovens, by-product plants and strip mills.

The town began to take shape during the 1860s incorporating three separate industrial settlements — Ebbw Vale, Beaufort and Victoria. From 1820 the Ebbw Vale Company had methodically planned housing for its workers providing long parallel rows of cottages. No shops were allowed, so people had to buy goods from the company's truck shops. In 1852 the company began to grant leases to builders and the first public building, the Literary and Scientific Institute, was finished in 1853. The company also built Christ Church in 1861 and the tower and spire were added in 1884-6.

The company's truck shops were abolished in 1872 and a new shopping quarter was built at Market Street and a market hall was completed in 1884. By 1900 the town had taken its present shape. The decline of the steelworks after the boom time of the war years was hastened by the rationalisation of the steel industry and the building of Llanwern steel sheet and strip mills on a more accessible shoreline site near Newport.

GROSMONT

Grosmont was formerly a small town which had a charter of incorporation and was administered by a mayor but today it is only a village. It lost its borough status in 1860, and with it the right to appoint a mayor and an ale taster. It is hidden in the folds of the hills, built on a south-facing slope which dips steeply down to a brook flowing in the valley bottom. Opposite is a hill called the Graig. Time seems to have passed Grosmont by, and although new houses have been built they have been sensitively sited so that the main street has an undisturbed quality. If one approaches by dropping down from Campstone Hill one sees an old yellow enamel AA sign giving the distance to London. The houses are strung out along the main street, the one side road having the unusual name 'Poorscript Lane'.

The heart of the village surrounds the Angel Hotel and the adjacent town hall. This stone-built hall was constructed in 1832 to replace a timbered hall on the same site. An inscription on the front records that it was presented to the parish together with the tolls by Henry, ninth Duke of Beaufort, in 1902. On the ground floor of the town hall is the toll stone; two veteran cars also shelter under its arches.

Opposite the post office, which is a few doors down from the pub, is a small lane that leads to Grosmont Castle (see chapter 4). On the lower side of the main street is the parish church of St Nicholas. This has a central eight-sided tower with a splendid spire, which, because the church is sited on the downhill slope from the village, barely rises above the roofline and chimney pots of the houses. It is a large church for such a small community so the nave and aisles are no longer used for services. The choir and transepts are separated from the rest of the church by a glazed screen and this provides sufficient space for the parishioners. The empty nave in the Early English style with sturdy circular columns can be seen to advantage. In this area of the church can be seen old agricultural machinery and memorial stones. An ancient cross bearing a simple carving of a mother and child, now much weathered, stands in the churchyard.

Grosmont is very much an agricultural village with working farms situated right in the centre.

LLANOVER

Llanover is a dispersed settlement with the old village and the parish church, dedicated to St Bartholomew, stretching along the banks of the river Usk. The main part of the village lies on the west side of the A4042, 4 miles (6 km) south of Abergavenny, with Llanover House and park enclosed by walls on the opposite side of the road. The core of the main settlement is the model village of Tre Elidyr, the whole of which is a unique memorial to heroes of the First World War. It was conceived by Lord Treowen, whose son and heir, Captain Elidyr Herbert, was killed on 17th November 1917 during active service in Palestine. Originally twenty houses were planned but only eighteen were built before Lord Treowen's own death (the last two have been built since). They surround a large village green on which stands the war memorial. This is an 11 foot (3.4 metre) high monolith with a gilded cross on top, behind which is a wall

The Town Hall, Grosmont.

bearing three brass plaques inscribed with the names of the fallen. The whole is set in a semicircle of lime trees, one for each man who died, with all their branches entwined.

On the far side of the green stands the village school, a one-storey building of classical design with the following words on the front: YSGOLDY TRE ELIDYR, YSGOL HARDWCH GWLAD. The second part is loosely translated as 'the school, the adornment of the country'.

The southern part of the village is composed of stone-built and white-washed houses which are scattered around a small valley through which runs the stream Rhyd-y-Meirch ('ford of the stallions'), which disappears under the road and re-emerges in the park. The water from this stream once provided the power for the Gwenffred woollen mill, which Lady Llanover set up in the nineteenth century to weave traditional Welsh flannel patterns. In one of the corners of the neat cottage gardens stands a traditional Welsh circular pig cot. Another can be seen in Upper Llanover.

Over the door of the village post office is a painting showing the Mari Llwyd (see chapter 9). It used to be a public house called the Nag's Head but Lady Llanover, who was a strict teetotaller, purchased all the taverns in the locality and converted them into coffee houses. The one exception is the Goose and Cuckoo, on the far boundary of the parish in Upper Llanover. So, unusually for a country village, Llanover has no pub at its centre.

On the north side of the village is the gatehouse (Porth Mawr) to Llanover Hall, which no longer exists. The house now known as Llanover House was originally the Dower House. The main mansion was demolished in 1935. The gateway, on its entrance side, has a tablet engraved with the following greeeting in Welsh:

'Who are thou comer?
If friend, the welcome of the heart to thee:
If stranger, hospitality shall meet thee:
If enemy, courtesy shall imprison thee.'
On the exit side, which visitors see when they leave, an inscription reads:
'Departing guests, leave a blessing,
On thy footsteps, and mayst though be blessed:
Health and prosperity be with thee on thy journey
And happiness on thy return.'

These verses were the winning entry for an eisteddfod competition set by Lady Llanover (see chapter 8). Unfortunately the stone has weathered and the inscriptions are difficult to read.

LLANTILIO CROSSENNY

Llantilio Crossenny lies in the rich rolling agricultural land of north-east Gwent. The name means 'the church of St Teilo at Iddon's Cross'. Iddon was a king in this area in the sixth century and legend has it that he prayed

51

to St Teilo to help defeat the plundering Saxons.

It is a small village of attractive cottages clustering around the parish church of St Teilo, which has a tall spire that towers above the village rooftops. It dates from the thirteenth century with later alterations in the Perpendicular and Decorated styles. The tower may be earlier than the nave as the arches of the crossing are considerably lower than normal. The shingled spire soaring above the tower and a peal of six bells were added in 1708-9. Enormous oak timbers to support the bells had to be inserted into the tower. The bells were recast in 1977 and a further two added. Other items of great interest in the church are a white marble memorial to Mary Anne Bosanquet, carved by Flaxman, a Norman font and, in the north chapel, two corbels carved with faces. Inside the porch stands an unusually large parish chest with three locks; it could be opened only when the vicar and both churchwardens were present. To circumvent

this arrangement the lid has been sawn so that one portion can be opened separately.

In the middle of the village is the Hostry, an ancient inn dating from 1459, with later additions. It would have provided refreshment for travellers going between Abergavenny and Monmouth. Since a more modern road has been constructed the village has become a quiet and peaceful place. It also has a small free school, situated at Brynderi, and founded by James Powell of The Court in 1654.

Near the church is Court Farm, which takes its name from 'Hen Gwrt' or Old Court, a medieval moated house some distance from the village, said to be the seat of David Gam, who was knighted by the king at Agincourt while dying from his wounds. While there is doubt that it belonged to David Gam, it certainly belonged to his son-in-law, Sir William ap Thomas of Raglan Castle, who married his daughter Gladys. David Gam is claimed by some to be Fluellen of Shakespeare's *Henry V*. Today there is no-

52

thing to be seen of the house. Where it stood there is now a thick carpet of grass surrounded by a water-filled moat gradually being taken over by bulrushes and wild flowers. It is a good site from which to view the tall spire of St Teilo's church surrounded by trees and the buildings of the village. From here one can follow the signs and go on to explore White Castle (see chapter 4).

LLANVIHANGEL CRUCORNEY

Llanvihangel Crucorney stands at the southern end of the Vale of Ewyas. At the end of the last ice age the glacier retreating up the valley left a small hill of moraine which diverted the Honddu brook, which now runs down the valley to flow northwards into the Monnow rather than into the Usk. It is on this low hill that most of the houses of Llanvihangel Crucorney are situated. Others are alongside the road which runs down from the hill and then on through the valley.

The village is mainly composed of stone-built houses, with a small church and the Skirrid Inn, which claims to be the oldest inn in Wales. It is said to have been the scene of hangings in medieval times but there are no architectural features earlier than the seventeenth century. In the church is a gravestone commemorating the village blacksmith who died in 1766; the epitaph reads:

'My sledge and hammer lies Reclin'd
Thy Bellows too have lost his Wind
My fires extinct, my Forge decay'd
And in ye Dust, my Vice is laid
My Coal is Spent, my Iron is gone
My nails Are drove, my Work is Done.'

The nave of the church is roofless and the walls form a courtyard joining the tower and the remainder of the church. With the sunlight streaming through the pink-tinted glass it is a warm and sheltered place to sit.

The Abergavenny to Hereford road, which used to run through the village, now separates it from the manor house, Llanvihangel Court (see chapter 6).

MATHERN

The name Mathern is a corruption of the name Merthyr Tewdric ('Tewdric the Martyr'). In the sixth century Mathern was a possession of the see of Llandaff. Tewdric, a ruler in the area, relinquished his sovereignty in favour of his son Meyric in order to live as a holy recluse. However, an unexpected invasion by the Saxons found Meyric deficient in the warrior qualities of his father. To avert disaster Tewdric returned to lead his people into battle in the vicinity of Tintern.

In the Book of Llandaff it is related that Tewdric was visited by an angel who foretold his victory but also his death 'by a single stroke in the district of the ford of Tintern', and that

he would 'in three days die in peace'. He was wounded by an enemy's lance, but Meyric's army was victorious. Tewdric died at Mathern, the place taking his name, which over the centuries has become the name we know today. The story is recorded on a tablet on the north wall of the chancel of the parish church, put there by Godwin, Bishop of Llandaff (1601-17). From the spot where he died immediately sprang a fountain of clear water which is today known as St Tewdric's Well (OS 162, ST 523910). Mathern church is supposed to have been built over his grave.

Before 1706 the Bishops of Llandaff had a palace in Mathern; it has since become a private house. It was built in the early fifteenth century during the bishopric of John de la Zouche (1408-16). Additions were made (including the chapel) during the occupancy of Bishop Miles Salley (1500-16), whose body was buried at Bristol although his will directed 'my heart and my bowells to be buried at the hygh altar in the church of Marthern befor Seynt Theodorycke'.

A stone tablet which once probably adorned the gateway to the bishop's palace, with a carving symbolising the Trinity flanked by angels, can now be seen in the National Museum of Wales.

MONMOUTH

Monmouth takes its name from the river Monnow, which flows into the Wye where the town has grown up. It was the Roman fort of *Blestium*. Between 1067 and 1071, during the Norman conquest, William Fitz Osbern established Monmouth Castle as one of a line of border forts. It had a commanding position protecting the double crossing of the Wye and the Monnow (see chapter 4). Before 1081 a chapel, shortly to become the priory church of St Mary, was founded. In 1086, when the Domesday Book was being compiled, Monmouth was treated ecclesiastically as part of Hereford and remained an English diocese until 1843; however, politically Monmouth was an independent Marcher Lordship. The castle stands on the highest part of a narrow neck of land formed by the converging courses of the Wye and the Monnow. On the north and west it has the natural protection of land falling away sharply to the Monnow. On the other sides an artificial ditch was cut. This was encroached on by back buildings and yards and its presence is reflected in the curve of the buildings fronting on to Agincourt Square.

The Norman borough was laid out on the ground sloping gradually towards the Wye and was defended by earthworks and palisades before walls were built in the late thirteenth and early fourteenth centuries. The course of the two rivers has determined the future growth of the town.

Great Castle House, Monmouth, was built in 1673.

The bridge which spans the Monnow is the only bridge in Britain with a fortified gatehouse. This dates from the second half of the thirteenth century. It was widened in the early nineteenth century by the addition of two walkways.

The market is held in Agincourt Square in the centre of the town. The square is surrounded by a number of handsome buildings of varying antiquity with the Shire Hall, built in 1724, at its centre. It is built in the classical style with an arcaded basement which gives shelter to the market traders. There is a cobbled square in front. In an arched recess on the front of the Shire Hall stands a statue, put up in 1792, of Henry V, who was born at Monmouth Castle in 1387. In front of the hall is a bronze figure of Charles Rolls (see chapter 8), designed by Sir William Goscombe John.

Monmouth Grammar School, now a public school, was founded by William Jones, who petitioned King James I in 1614 to establish a school and an almshouse to maintain twenty poor people. William Jones made his fortune as a haberdasher after having run away to London because he was unable to pay a debt of ten groats.

Monmouth is also famous for the 'Monmouth cap', a knitted hat referred to in Shakespeare's *Henry V*. It is thought that Over Monnow, separated from the town by the Monnow bridge, was the centre of the cap-making industry.

NEWPORT

Newport is the largest town in the county. It grew up where the Usk flows into the Bristol Channel and as its name suggests it is a port. The Normans established a castle on the banks of the river to control the crossing and boats going up and down the river. All that remains today is the eastern wall of the castle, which has three towers, the middle one having a water gate through which small vessels could enter. A dual carriageway has been built over the site of the western part of the castle. Although it is now in public care, the castle is difficult to view as it is surrounded by a bridge, the new road and the river.

Near this fortress a town grew up which is first mentioned in documents about 1126 when it was called 'Novus Burgus', suggesting that there was previously no Welsh settlement on the site. The town was walled (there is no evidence remaining today) with two gates; the east gate was somewhere in the present High Street and the west gate was at the bottom of Stow Hill and is remembered today in the name of Westgate Hotel.

The town did not grow much from medieval times until the nineteenth century and was little more than one street running from the castle and wooden bridge to the church of St Woolos (see chapter 5). Visitors to the town recorded it as being poor, with ill-paved and dirty streets.

The town began to grow rapidly with the industrialisation of the valleys, when Newport became the centre of export for vast quantities of iron and coal. The opening of the Monmouthshire Canal in 1796 began this growth and later the railway, which came to Newport in 1850 and superseded the canal as the major freight carrier, ensured that it continued.

The canal reached the Town Pill just below the bridge; wharves and slipways extended all along the right-hand bank of the river. The names of the wharves still exist but only a few are used today, by sand and gravel boats.

As a result of the overwhelming demand for river wharf space, the canal was extended to the present docks area, which was completed in the 1840s. To illustrate the importance of this period in the history of Newport the Green Crossing murals were commissioned in 1971. They are situated in a pedestrian underpass near the castle. The mosaic was designed by Kenneth Budd and completed in 1975. It shows a scene of about 1851-3 with railway locomotives and horse-drawn canal boats against a portside background.

A prominent feature of the docks area is the unusual transporter bridge, which was opened in 1906 by Lord Tredegar. It was built to improve the access to the east bank of the Usk where the Orb Steelworks was situated. The closely spaced piers of a conventional swing or lifting bridge would have hampered shipping, so an aerial ferry was chosen. It was designed by F. Arnodin, who was responsible for a similar bridge in Rouen. A gondola is suspended from a trolley propelled by a continuous cable and is capable of carrying 35 tons.

There are many fine Victorian and Edwardian buildings in the town dating from Newport's heyday but one timber-framed Tudor building in High Street worthy of mention is the Murenger House. The 'murenger' was responsible for collecting and administering the 'murage' or wall tolls, which paid for the construction and maintenance of the town's defences. If the post of murenger ever existed in Newport, it terminated long before the date inscribed on the building.

Newport also has a modern shopping centre built in the 1960s and 1970s and centring around John Frost Square, where Newport Museum and Art Gallery (see chapter 6) is located. John Frost was mayor of Newport in the early nineteenth century and became famous for leading the Chartist demonstration to Newport (see chapter 8), which led to a riot in which 22 people were killed. Another mural on the walls of the shopping precinct illustrates this event.

The transporter bridge constructed in 1906, Newport.

Newport Docks in 1906.

The Civic Centre, which dominates the town, was started in 1937. It was designed by T. C. Howitt and Partners of Nottingham. The clock tower, marble staircase and entrance hall, which were all part of the original design, were completed during the 1960s. It houses the assize and county court and magistrates' courts. Inside, the building is decorated with murals painted by Hans Feibush in 1961-4, showing events in the history of the county.

PONTYPOOL

Pontypool (meaning either 'the bridge of the pool' or 'Pont ap Howel') was once an important centre of the coal and iron trade. The manufacture of iron was started about 1425 at Pontymoel; however, the area did not develop until Richard Hanbury purchased land there in 1588 for ironmaking. The Hanbury family played an enormous part in the history and development of the town and they lived at Pontypool Park House from the late seventeeth century until 1915.

Pontypool Park House was originally built in 1690-1720 but was later substantially improved and expanded by Capel Hanbury Leigh between 1779 and 1840, while retaining the earlier facade. He was able to afford these improvements from increased profits due to greater demand for munitions during the wars with France between 1793 and 1815. Around the house 158 acres (64 ha) were enclosed as a park. Much of the work done on the house and gardens is said to have been the inspiration of Capel's first wife, Molly Anne Mackworth. She designed the grotto in the park (which can be seen by appointment with the Valley Inheritance Centre). It was built in the 1830s and is decorated with shells and stones and has fine views over the Usk valley. Other interesting things in the park are the imposing park gates, the National Eisteddfod stone circle (1924) and a dry ski slope. The house today is a Roman Catholic comprehensive school and the stable block behind has been converted into a museum (see chapter 6). Opposite the entrance to the museum can be seen the remains of the ice house which stored ice for the Hanbury household.

Pontypool is also a market town. The Old Corn Market in George Street was built in 1731 by Miss Frances Bray. It is now occupied by shops but still has the family arms on the facade. The present market was built in 1891 by the architect Robert Williams. The Town Hall was presented to Pontypool by Capel Hanbury Leigh to commemorate the birth of his son and heir in 1853 when he himself was 77 years old.

Pontypool is also famous for the manufacture of Japan ware which became known as Pontypool Japan ware. It was begun in the late seventeenth century by Thomas Allgood, who developed a process to coat iron goods and decorate them in the fashionable Japanese lacquered style. The method was a closely guarded secret and died with the family. The ware is now highly prized. A fine display can be seen at the National Museum of Wales.

Pontypool was the first place where flag days were held. They were started by a local lady, Mrs Edith George, in 1914 when she made flags of red, white and blue on matchsticks to raise money for the troops' comfort fund. In the first year £10 was raised but by the end of the First World War £35 million was collected by the same method.

Today Pontypool is perhaps best known for its rugby club, which was established in 1901.

RAGLAN

Raglan's most important building is the magnificent castle (see chapter 4), although it is about half a mile (800 metres) from the village, which centres around several inns, shops and St Cadoc's church. The church dates from the fourteenth century but was built on an earlier, tenth-century site. The Beauforts added a north chapel, where many of the Somerset family lie. A notice in the church commemorates a visit in 1946 by the Institute of Mechanical Engineers 'to the scene and resting place of Edward Somerset 2nd Marquis of Worcester who gave the world the first practical steam engine . . .' (see chapter 8). The clock on the church tower has only three faces because Miss Anna Maria Bosanquet, the donor, forbade a fourth as it would have faced the railway station (which no longer exists), of which she disapproved.

In the High Street are Old Courthouse, formerly a magistrates' court and now a restaurant, and the Ship Inn, the name being a corruption of 'sheep'. A market was once held on the cobbled forecourt. On Chepstow Road stands the school built in 1857 by the Duke of Beaufort. In Beaufort Square is the stone base of the original market cross, which now acts as a base for a lamp post. Today Raglan is a mainly residential village for people who work elsewhere.

SKENFRITH

Skenfrith stands on the old Abergavenny to Ross-on-Wye road but since a new road has been built it has been bypassed by modern development and the only continuous noise is provided by water rushing over the weir. It is a single-street village running parallel to the river Monnow, which meanders under an attractive three-arched stone bridge and around the wooded slopes of Coed-anghred hill. The name of the village is probably a corruption of Ynys Cynfraeth, derived from the name of a sixth-century chieftain.

The church is dedicated to St Bridget or St

58

Pontypool Park gates, made in the 1720s, were remodelled in 1835 by Thomas Deakin.

Bride (see chapter 5) and stands not far from the castle (see chapter 4). There is a green around the castle and opposite, attached to the village stores, is the Moat House, a reminder that instead of the village green there used to be a moat surrounding the castle. On the other side the castle is protected by the Monnow and a leat which diverts water to power the mill, part of which has been built into the castle walls. The mill has been restored to full working order and one can purchase stone-ground flour there.

The Waen, a manor house in the sixteenth century, now a farmhouse, was the home of John Philip Morgan, whose monument can be seen in the church. He was the last constable of the castle and a member of Parliament for Monmouthshire in 1553-4. His brother, Sir Richard Morgan of Blackbrook, was the judge who sentenced Lady Jane Grey to death. It so affected his conscience that he lost his reason.

At the far end of the village is the National School built in 1843 and now the village hall. On the main road stands the Bell Inn and close by is a water trough so that both people and animals could refresh themselves on a journey.

TREDEGAR

Tredegar extends north to south along the Sirhowy valley from the Heads of the Valleys road. It was a former ironworks town that later

turned to coal mining. These heavy industries have now largely disappeared.

The first industrialised part was the northern end of the Sirhowy valley, where in 1778 a furnace was established. It was the first in Gwent to be fired with coke. The first furnace to be established in Tredegar itself was built by Samuel Homfray in 1801. He was son-in-law to Sir Charles Morgan of Tredegar House near Newport and the Tredegar Ironworks was named in his honour, thus giving the town its name.

The town is well laid out with streets radiating from The Circle (originally called Market Square), where the clock tower, Tredegar's most famous landmark, stands. Both clock and tower are in iron and are a reminder of the town's origin and growth based on the iron industry. The idea for the clock came from Mrs Davies, wife of the Tredegar Ironworks manager, who lived at Bedwellty House. She took a keen interest in the affairs of the town and her husband offered a donation of £400 if she could raise the remainder. A committee was formed and preparations to hold a bazaar were made. Mrs Davies died before the event was held, but the money raised, together with a further contribution by Mr Davies, reached the target figure of £1000. The clock was designed by J. B. Joyce of Shropshire, while the engineer

59

James Watson was responsible for the overall design of the tower and oversaw its completion. It was cast at the iron foundry of Charles Jordan in Newport and was erected in 1859.

Downhill from the clock tower is Bedwellty House, standing in a park which was given to the town in 1901 by Lord Tredegar. It is an early nineteenth-century house which belonged to the ironmasters. It is now used as municipal offices but also has some museum displays inside, which can be viewed by appointment. In the main chamber can also be seen a bust of Aneurin Bevan (see chapter 8), whose memorial stones stand on the hillside just outside the town. Amongst items of interest in the grounds of the house is a 15 ton block of coal, the largest hand-hewn piece in the world. It was cut for the 1851 Great Exhibition. There is also an ice house and a handsome Victorian bandstand.

TRELLECK

Trelleck means 'stone town' and derives its name from three standing stones, sometimes called Harold's Stones, just outside the village. They are said to have been put up to commemorate one of King Harold's conquests but they are much earlier than this, although their original purpose is unknown. They may have

The clock tower in 'The Circle', Tredegar.

been way markers or for religious purposes.

In medieval times Trelleck was a borough with a mayor and burgesses and a market, but it declined and by 1700 it was described as being 'now reduced to a poore inconsiderable village'. The large church (see chapter 5), which stands in the centre of the village, is a reminder that the settlement was once wealthier than it is today.

Inside the church is an interesting stone sundial which formerly stood in the school grounds. It was put up by Magdalen, the widow of Sir George Probert of Pantglas, in 1689. Not only is it a sundial but it also points out things of interest in the village. The sides of the sundial's pedestal show the Terret Tump, the three standing stones and the Virtuous Well. When the pedestal was moved from its original position it was found to be an ancient font from the church.

Terret Tump stands at the rear of Court Farm and is an immense artificial mound which was the motte of a Norman fortification. It may have got its name from the fact that it once had a 'turret' on top.

The Virtuous Well is in a field to the south-east of the village. It is enclosed and has stone seating. The water from two or three springs empties into the basin and is supposed to have healing properties.

Many of the houses in the village date from the seventeenth, eighteenth and early nineteenth centuries and are built of the local pudding stone, a quartz conglomerate. The two pubs, the Crown Inn and the Lion, served travellers journeying on the Monmouth to Chepstow road.

USK

Usk was the Roman legionary fort of *Burrium*, constructed from AD 55 to about AD 75. *Burrium* was reduced in size by constructing a small fort within the original defences. The soldiers were transferred to construct the large new fort at Caerleon (*Isca*). This move may have been caused by the severe flooding from the river Usk which the town periodically experiences.

The smaller fort remained in use until the end of the second century and then *Burrium* continued as a thriving industrial settlement protected by an earth bank and ditch, known as Clawdd Du. *Burrium* ceased to be occupied by the Romans when they withdrew from Britain at the end of the fourth century.

After this little is known about the settlement of Usk until the twelfth century. Though the Priory Church (see chapter 5) appears to be of earlier date, the first documentary mention of the town dates from 1131.

The name Usk is an anglicised form of the Celtic *Wysg*, which denotes the river on which the town stands. Usk is also known by the

Bridge Street, Usk.

name of *Bryn-Buga*, which can be seen on modern signposts; however, the origin of this name is uncertain.

The strategic significance of Usk was re-established by the Normans, who constructed the castle in the eleventh century. It was rebuilt in stone in the twelfth century with important additions in the thirteenth and fourteenth centuries. The de Clare family owned the castle for 200 years and played an important role in local affairs leading to the foundation of a Benedictine priory (estab-lished by 1236), the creation of an autonomous Lordship of Usk in 1245 from the larger Lordship of Striguil and the formation of the borough in 1397.

Usk Castle was the scene of considerable fighting during the middle ages but was re-corded as being in ruins in 1587. It was purchased by the Duke of Beaufort in 1750 and it was probably at this time that the old gatehouse was converted into the dwelling known today as Castle House. The castle remains in private hands today.

Unusually, Usk has two squares. Twyn Square (*twyn* means hillock, which suggests that an earth mound or tumulus may once have existed on the site) was the original site of the market, which was transferred to New Market Street in 1598. The clock tower in the centre was put up in 1887 for Queen Victoria's Golden Jubilee.

In the middle of New Market Street stands the old Town Hall, which is substantially as it was built by the Duke of Beaufort in 1771. The blocked arches of the ground floor could be the remains of the seventeenth-century hall. The lower part of the block facing up the street was added in the early nineteenth century in the Palladian style.

Usk has a number of attractive houses dating from the fifteenth century to the present day. Great House in Old Market Street dates from the fifteenth century but was subdivided into several dwellings in the eighteenth century. The Malt Barn, now housing a museum (see chapter 6), may also have been a wealthy merchant's house dating from the fifteenth century.

Another substantial and formidable building in the town stands in Newgate Street. Originally it was built as a house of correction in 1842 at a cost of £22,000. It is now used for young offenders. However, this building does not detract from the considerable charm of the town.

11
Tourist information centres

Abergavenny: 2 Lower Monk Street. Telephone: Abergavenny (0873) 3254 or 77588. Seasonal opening.
Blaenavon: Big Pit Mining Museum. Telephone: Blaenavon (0495) 790122. Seasonal opening.
Chepstow: The Gatehouse, High Street. Telephone: Chepstow (029 12) 3772. Seasonal opening.
Cross Keys: Cwmcarn Forest Drive Entrance. Telephone: Cross Keys (0495) 272001. Seasonal opening.
Monmouth: Church Street. Telephone: Monmouth (0600) 3899.
Newport: Newport Museum and Art Gallery, John Frost Square. Telephone: Newport (0633) 842962.
Tintern: Tintern Abbey. Telephone: Tintern (029 18) 431.

GWENT

* Countryside sites (Ch.2)
⊓ Places of archaeological interest (Ch.3)
C Castles (Ch.4)
+ Churches, chapels (Ch.5)
A Monastic ruin (Ch.5)
M Museum (Ch.6)
▲ Historic house (Ch.6)
I Industrial history (Ch.7)
■ Town, village (Ch.10)

A *Llanthony Priory*

+ Cwmyoy

C■ Grosmont

R.Monnow

⊓ *Twyn-y-Gaer*
■ *Llanvihangel Crucorney*

+ Skenfrith
C

▲ *Llanvihangel Court*

BRECON *BEACONS
NATIONAL PARK

R.Usk

C *White Castle*
■ Llantilio Crossenny

C M MONMOUTH
R.Wye
* Kymin

Clydach Valley I
M+
C ■ ABERGAVENNY

■ BRYNMAWR

Clytha
* *Picnic Site*

C
■ Raglan

Sirhowy Ironworks I
■ Nantyglo
■ EBBW VALE
■ TREDEGAR   ■ Blaina

I+
M ■ BLAENAVON
■ Llanover
+ Llanvair Kilgeddin
+ Bettws Newydd

I *Forge Row*

Trelleck ⊓ ■
+

Cwmtillery Lake *
I *Cwmbyrgwm Water Balance Pit*

Broadmeend *

Tintern A
Abbey * I

Pen-y-Fan Pond *

M ■ PONTYPOOL
+ ■ USK
M
▲ *Junction Cottage*

* *Beaufort Aviaries*

+ Llangwm
Wyndcliff *

I Crumlin
Mountain Air *
■ *Llandegfedd Reservoir*

M *Wolvesnewton Model Farm*

Blackwood ■

Cwmcarn Forest Drive *
Farm Park

Gaer Llwyd ⊓

⊓ *Llanmellin*
CHEPSTOW ■
M C +

M ■ CWMBRAN

R.Usk

⊓ *Gray Hill*

Wentwood Reservoir *
C *Penhow Castle*

⊓ *Twm Barlwm*

C *Caerwent* ■ ⊓

M4

■ Mathern
⊓ *Heston Brake*
I *Sudbrook*

Cwmfelinfach +
Sirhowy Valley *
Country Park

M Risca

M
C ■ CAERLEON

CM
Caldicot

Fourteen Locks I

Gwern-
y-Cleppa ⊓

+ ■
M NEWPORT

▲ *Tredegar House*

Druidstone ⊓

M4

Index

Page numbers in italic refer to illustrations.